AF519670

Ethnic Unrests and India's Security Concerns

ETHNIC UNRESTS AND INDIA'S SECURITY CONCERNS

Kashinathn Jena
Bindu Ranjan Chakma

ABHIJEET PUBLICATIONS
DELHI 110094

ABHIJEET PUBLICATIONS
2/46 Tukhmeerpur Extension
Delhi 110094
Phones: 011-22960492, 65698474
e-mail: abhijeetpublication@gmail.com
abhijeet_singh1@indiatimes.com

ETHNIC UNRESTS AND INDIA'S SECURITY CONCERNS

First Published 2008

© Authors

ISBN 978-81-89886-30-1

Price: Rs. 380/- (INR)

[All rights reserved. No part of this publication may be reproduced, copied, stored in a retrieval system, transmitted or used in any form or by any means, whether electronic, mechanical, photocopying, recording or otherwise, without the prior permission from the author or publisher, except for a brief quotations in critical articles or reviews.

PRINTED IN INDIA

Published by J.K. Singh fo Abhijeet Publications, Delhi 110094, Lasertypeset by Gaurav Graphics, Delhi and Printed as Himanshu Printers, Delhi.

Acknowledgements

This book is based mainly on content analysis of selected documents of both historical and contemporary books with the application of inductive methodology. For this purpose, a number of interviews have been taken from journalists, academicians, social scientist, socio-political activists, research scholars, policy makers and administrators who have in depth knowledge and orientation in ethnic studies in general and the CHT, political crisis in particular. This has been taken in the CHT, Tripura, Kolkatta & New Delhi. For this we are greatly indebted to all those personalities.

For writing this book we have received constant encouragement, support & co-operation from many corners. Our thanks and acknowledgement are due for all of them. Here, we are specially indebted to our colleagues in respective work places. Again in the course of writing this book, we have visited and used the facilities of a number of libraries in Delhi, Kolkata, Hyderabad and Shimla. Hence we are immensely thankful to the staff of the libraries of

Institute of Defense and Strategic Analysis (IDSA), Delhi, Department of International Relations of Jadavpur Universities, Kolkata, American Studies Research Center (ASRC), Hyderabad, Indian Institute of Advanced Study, Shimla for their kind assistance and co-operation in collaboration by extending access to required books in the libraries. We are also thankful to Mr. Subir Bhaumik, Mr. Bhabatosh Dewan, and Mr. Ravi Das Chakma who provided us with some useful documents for writing the second and third chapters of books.

We are also extremely indebted to Prof. Arunoday Saha, Hon. Vice-Chancellor of Tripura University and Dr. H.S. Chakraborty, Deputy Librarian of Tripura University for their constructive and constant encouragement for undertaking and completing this work.

Dr. Kashinath Jena
Reader, Dept. Pol. Science
Tripura University

Bindu Ranjan Chakma
Asst. Professor, Dept. of Pol. Science
Netaji Subhash Mahavidlaya, Tripura

Abbreviations

ATTF-	All Tripura Tiger Force
MNF-	Mizo National Front
MULTA-	Muslim United Liberation Front of Assam
NDFB-	National Democratic Front of Bodoland
NLFT-	National Liberation Front of Tripura
NSCN-IM-	Nationalist Socialist Council of Nagaland (Issac-Muivah)
NSCN-K-	Nationalist Socialist Council of Nagaland (Kaplang)
PCJSS-	Parbattya Chattagram Jana Sanghati Samiti
PLA-	Peoples Liberation Army
ULFA-	United Liberation Front of Assam
UNLF-	United National Liberation Front
UNPO-	Unrepresented Peoples Organization
UPDF-	United Peoples Democratic Front

Contents

1

Introduction and Conceptual Basis

The Chittagong Hill Tracts (CHT) political crisis of Bangladesh is one of the oldest ethnic problems in the post-colonial reconstruction of the South Asian nation states. The rise of ethnic insurgency in the second half of 1970s, tight militarization of the CHT, implantation of thousands of Muslim settlers from different plain districts of Bangladesh and communalization of politics in the CHT led to grave deterioration in the law and order situation of the region. The 'Jummas'[1] were in favor the CHT's integration with the Union of India during partition of the Indian sub-continent.[2] The Jummas also share ethnic and cultural linkages with communities living in many Northeastern Indian states, particularly in Mizoram and Tripura.[3] Moreover, the CHT being geographically in proximity with Mizoram and Tripura, these two Indian states, more particularly the later one faced the problem of refugee influx from the CHT, whenever its political environment turned worse. This development urged India, if not directly, to expand indirectly its influence into the area. The Bangladesh's security establishment, particularly in the post-Mujib era did not see it positively. Instead, it developed apprehension and misperception about India's motive in the CHT. The bilateral relations between India and Bangladesh severely deteriorated in the post-Mujib era. All these developments encouraged the hardliners of Bangladesh's security establishment to adopt a strategy, that encourages backing the anti Indian obscurantist elements and allow them to use its soil (particularly the CHT) in planning and execution of their subversive operations against India (discussed more in details in the third chapter).

A peace accord was signed between the Parbattya Chattagram Jana Sanghati Shamiti (PCJSS)[4] and the Government of Bangladesh (GoB) on December 2, 1997 with a view to re-establish political stability and peace in the CHT. However, political cleavages between the JSS and the United Peoples Democratic Front (UPDF)[5] continued unabated in the post accord situation of the CHT. In such an ugly political environment, the Awami League (AL) and the Bangladesh Nationalist Party (BNP), the two main political parties of Bangladesh politicized the peace accord from their own strategic point of view. Finally, lack of sincerity on the part of the GoB in implementation of the peace accord further exacerbated the post accord situation of the CHT thereby making it more complicated and explosive in nature. In other words, the CHT political crisis continues to be a major problem.

The primary objective of this book is not to look at the national security problem of Bangladesh, which is emanated from ethnic insurgency and political movement of the Jummas in the CHT. It rather focuses on how a national political problem of Bangladesh like the CHT political crisis impinges on India's national security. Undertaking an analytical work in such area is significant not only because of lacuna in the existing literature on the subject, but because of intractable nature of the CHT political crisis in the near future.

The book locates the areas where the CHT political crisis threatens India's national security. Chapter 1 of the book exclusively analyzes this problem. Besides locating this problem, the introductory part also attempts to define 'security' dealing with the major theoretical approaches, identifies India's present national security interests and major security issues, and succinctly deals with the intellectual debate in India over the means through which India can promote its national interests by overcoming the security challenges. The second chapter endeavors to trace in brief the genesis of the CHT political crisis and the political movement of the Jummas by addressing the root causes of the problem. It argues that a long-term solution of the CHT political crisis, GoB needs to address the causes of fear, apprehension and suspicion among the Jummas. It argues that spread of communitarian values and a national political consensus among the major political parties of Bangladesh are very important to overcome this problem. Chapter four analyses India's CHT policy. Here it argues, India paid more attention to its preferred economic and political interests and moved through regional and extra-regional geo-strategic calculation. Therefore, the government of India went on ignoring the security threat posed by the CHT political crisis. The conclusion of the dissertation argues that the CHT political crisis requires a permanent solution for national security interests of both India and Bangladesh. Bilateral initiative addressing the root causes of the problem can play an effective role in this regard without compromising the core national interests of both the nations- India and Bangladesh.

Conceptual Basis: Dimensions of Security

In international relations (IR), the primary objective of very nation is protect and promote its national interests and guard national security against any possible external encroachment. What is 'security?

Territorial integrity without full sovereignty or sovereignty without full territorial integrity can never be considered true security.[6] (Janayantanuja Bandhyopadhyaya)

A nation in the international system is secure only when it is capable of maintaining its independent identity and territorial integrity.[7] (Bary Buzan)

Sometimes many nations compel to surrender their sovereignty to a considerable extent either through treaties, agreements or simply because of the domination of a powerful state on a comparatively less powerful state even without loosing territorial integrity. For instance, many West and the East European nations, during the Cold-War period compromised their sovereignty to the US and the USSR respectively partly due to the strong domination by the later, albeit these states did not lose their territorial integrity. Similarly, 'territorial integrity is also partially lost without endangering sovereignty. For example, India lost some of her territory to China between 1959 and 1962 without endangering its sovereignty.[8]

Therefore, 'security' does not only mean preservation of territorial integrity or boundaries of the state but it also includes maintenance independent identity and functional integrity of a state at the external environment.

For Walter Lippmann, security means preservation of core values of a state by any means. He says,

> A nation is secured to the extent to which it is not in danger of having to sacrifice core values, if it wishes to avoid war, and is able, if challenged, to maintain them by victory in such a war.[9]

Lippmann's definition is not free from shortcomings. Only the powerful nations have the capabilities to preserve the core values by victory in war, and such victory is certain only when it is fought against a comparatively less powerful state. The US's victory in the recent wars in Afghanistan and Iraq has been possible only due to high military superiority of the US over these two states. Similarly, when the problem is between two equally powerful states with equal nuclear strike capability, waging war is not an easy task even when the enemy nation encroaches some of its core values. For instance, despite knowing the fact that Pakistan attacks its core values like democracy, secularism in diverge ways, India could not wage a full-fledged war against Pakistan in the post Pokharan-II, because Pakistan attained nuclear parity and second strike capability against India. Sometimes, a strong anti war international public opinion also stands as an impediment to declare a highly escalated war against an adversary.

Non-Military Dimension of Security

There are also many, who argue that the notion of security study remains inadequate without considering the non-military and human aspects of security.[10] Sometimes, a state fails to provide security to the lives and properties of the people. People's agitation against the existing state's apparatus reaches at peak. Political instability arising out of such situation makes the state not only externally weak, but in extreme cases, throws it into territorial disintegration. The case of the former USSR is a classic example in this regard. Considering all these aspects, security could be said to consist of

i. preservation of territorial integrity and sovereignty,

ii. preservation of core values,

iii. promotion of peripheral interests which vary from state to state and from time to time depending the relative capabilities of the nation states and circumstances,

iv. providing security to the lives and properties of the people.

Ethnicity and the Problem of National Integration

All the major South Asian states face the problem of ethnic conflicts. Sri Lanka faces the problem of political and geo-graphical integration in the Northeastern parts, where the LTTE has been waging a war against the Sinhalese dominated Sri Lankan Government for a separate political entity for the Tamil people. India faces similar problem in many of the Northeastern states like Assam, Tripura, Manipur, Nagaland, Maghalaya and in Jammu and Kashmir. Ethnic insurgency in the CHT is a major problem of Bangladesh. Similarly, Pakistan faces such problem in Karachi, Baluchistan. Infact, ethnic problem is one of the major problems in the postcolonial reconstruction of the South Asian states. This problem has a regional dimension because most of the South Asian states are victims of this problem. The ethnic problem of one state has link to the ethnic problems of other states due to cultural and linguistic proximity between people of these states. Therefore, it is a threat to the security, both military and non-military, of the both parties. For example, the political crisis has its link to the ethnic insurgency in the Northeast of India. Therefore, it impinges not only on the security of Bangladesh, but also on the security of India, which has been analyzed in details in chapter three. Ethnic nationalism and ethnic insurgency may not pose a serious military threat, but it continues to be a major threat to human security and promotion of good governance.

Security: Different Theoretical Perspective

What are the survival strategies of the nation states in the domain of international relations? How far does military power ensure national integrity and core values of a state? Is security is an interdependent concept among numerous actors of our international system? What is the functional role of international institutions? How far have the international institutions like the UNO, the WTO been successful in achieving their functional objectives? To address the above questions, we need to look at contemporary theories, which exclusively deal with the concept of 'security'.

The realist school of thought argues that international political system is always anarchic in nature.[11] Political realism holds the views that there is constant clash of interests among the actors in the international system and in such an anarchic environment, the states have to depend on their relative powers for ensuring their survival and other vital national interests. As classical realist, Hans J. Morgenthau says:

> A political policy seeks either to keep power, to increase power or to demonstrate power. A nation, whose foreign policy tends towards keeping power and not towards changing the distribution of power in its favor pursues a policy status quo. A nation whose policy seeks a favorable change in power status seeks a policy of imperialism. A nation policy that seeks to demonstrate the power it has, either for maintaining it, pursues a policy of prestige.[12]

Morgenthau's observation carries significant in many respects. For instance, in the politics of South Asia, India is determined to preserve its status quo as a regional power. Similarly, interalia other objectives, the US's post 9/11 military demonstrations in Afghanistan and Iraq have been motivated to a considerable extent for regaining back its military prestige lost during 9/11 incident.

The neo-realists assume, uncertainty arising out of

miscalculation and distrust is inherent in the international system whether it is bi-polar, multi-polar or uni-polar in nature. According to Kenneth Waltz, although the behavior of the nation states changes with change in international systemic order and resultant shift in distribution of capability among the actors, the functional objective i.e. ensuring survival and other vital interests remain unchanged. However, every state, as Waltz says, always remains concerned about its relative power before taking any political action.[13]

Therefore, according to the realists, power is the most decisive force that determines the foreign policy orientation of a state. What do the realists mean by the term 'power'?

By the term 'power,' the realists generally mean military capabilities.[14] In international relations, power means the relative ability of one actor to influence the behavior of the other actors. According to Robert A Dahl, power means the ability to shift the probability of outcomes. He explains it in the following language:

> When A is believed to have power over B, A can surely get B to do something, which B would not otherwise do.[15]

Scharzenber is another scholar who also defined power similarly. In his words,

> Power means *capacity to impose one's will on other by reliance on effective sanctions in case of non-compliance.*[16]

From the above discussion, we can briefly highlight political realism in the following points:

i. The realists are primary concerned about national security.

ii. Military power is the most vital force in ensuring national security,

iii. As there is constant clash of interests among the actors in the international system, they are very pessimistic about international co-operation among them. International relations are a prisoner's dilemma game. Therefore, cooperation among the actors arises only out of the dilemmas of common aversion and common interests.[17]

Contrary to the realist's assumption on 'security', institutionalists and the neo-liberalists argue that the concept of security is interdependence among the actors, and this is relevant particularly in the era of globalization. They hold the view that institutionalized form of co-operation helps governs the anarchic international system better and provides wider scope for international peace and ensures more the security of the nation states.[18]

Democratic peace theory, another liberal approach to the study of international security, argues that spread of democratic values, ideological commitment to human rights and transnational interdependence can promote and maintain better international security.[19]

International institutions like the UNO, the WTO, and arms control regimes such as the Missile Technology Control Regime (MTCR), Fissile Material Cut of Treaty (FMCT), and Nuclear Non-Proliferation

Treaty (NPT), regional institutions like the European Union (EU), Association of South-East Asian Nations (ASEAN) etc. have of-course contributed widely in promoting international co-operation among the nation-states. For instance, the UNO provided good offices, from time to time, as means for pacific settlement of international and regional disputes (e.g. Indo-Pakistan conflict over Kashmir, Arab-Israeli conflict over West Bank, Gaza Strip etc.). It has been successful in containing escalation of many conflicts in many war torn areas like Lebanon, Yemen, Congo, Cyprus, Rwanda etc. by conducting peacekeeping operations. Similarly, the WTO with 150 member countries is now one of the most powerful global institutions with executive, legislative and judicial authority. It has a 'Dispute Settlement Body' (DSP) for pacific settlement of trade-related disputes arising among the member-states.

Yet, at another level we find, these global institutions have failed largely to enforce their rules effectively especially when the interests of the big powers were involved. For example, the UN Security Council, the principal peace-enforcing agency of the UN, lost its usefulness and creditability, when the US, without its endorsement, intervened in the Korean crisis (1950-53) and very recently in Iraq. Similarly, the WTO has failed to secure the US's ratification to the Kyoto protocol, albeit, the US's ratification is essential for preserving our bio-diversity and eco-inhabitation.

According to the realists, the failure of these two global institutions in effective enforcement of these principles is pre-eminent because these institutions remain under the control of the powerful states. Therefore, they primarily function to promote the global interests of these powerful states. Kenneth Waltz strongly argues that concept of globalization is originated in the US. Naturally, all current institutions and rules that sustain and promote global economy are under American control.[20]

Waltz's observation on 'globalization' is significant in many respects. WTO, the principal rule making body of the globalization process incorporates all the original treaty provisions of the Dunkel's proposals or General Agreement on Tariffs and Trade (GATT). The agreements on agriculture (AOA), intellectual property rights (TRIPs) and trade related investment (TRIMs) under the WTO regime promote global economic interests of the Northern Developed Nations in general and USA in particular.[21] Out of the 500 largest MNCs, that play the key role in the globalization process, 441 are located in the Triad (NAFTA, which is under the US domination, EU and Japan), and only 14 outside the OECD countries.[22]

Realists also argue that institutionalization and conceptualization of regimes is interest based. As a result, a shift in the pattern interests and preferences of the actors, which is resulted from international systemic change, brings a change either in the regime or an end in it entirely.[23]

The critical theorists, on the other hand, believe that security is assured better only through human emancipation and when it is understood in terms of freeing people as individuals and groups from social, physical, economic, political and other constrains that stop them from carrying out what they freely chose to do.[24]

The post-modernists emphasize on re-conceptualization of the term 'security' by replacing realism with a communitarian discourse. They believe that the 'post-modern epistemic community' can help overcoming the traditional security dilemma by spreading communitarian values.[25]

Social constructivism, another approach to the study of international relations, emphasizes on bridging the gap between rationalism (neo-realism and neo-liberalism) and reflectivism (post-modernism, critical theory, normative theory etc.). The social constructivist thinkers argue that the fundamental structures of international politics are socially constructed and a change in our way of thinking can create a scope for greater international security. A 'security community', which emphasizes on shared knowledge and maintains trust in it, can resolve international disputes without war.[26]

Security Dilemma in the 21st Century

Following the end of the Cold War, there was anticipation that a paradigmatic shift in security studies was likely to occur in international relations. Globalization would mitigate military competition and conflict through the process of institutionalized form of cooperation. The increasing trend in the globalization process and institutionalized forms of cooperation (CBMs both military and non-military) have undoubtedly played significant role in lessening down the competitive aspects of the security dilemma between states. ASEAN Regional Forum (ARF), which looks after ASEAN as well as trans-ASEAN regional security issues, is a classic example of institutionalized form of cooperation. Similarly, CBMs between India and China helped them overcoming their mutual distrust to a considerable extent.

However, on the other hand, we find, nuclear powers, although emphasize on nuclear non-proliferation, continue to enhance the quality of their nuclear strike capability through computer simulation tests and other sophisticated techniques. The nuclear tests conducted by India and Pakistan in 1998, USA's determination in deploying a National Missile Defense System (NMD) against 'rogue!' states and opposition by both Russia and China indicate that the national security interests continue to maintain its importance in the beginning of the new century. The recent Iraq war without endorsement of the UN mechanism has further reflected a lack of consensus among the actors in generating cooperative security ideas. Therefore, traditional security ambiguity with mutual distrust, apprehension and suspicion continues to dominate the behavior of the nation states in the domain of international relation's in the beginning of the 21st century.

National Interests, Security Issues and Security Policy of India

National interests with the acceptation of the core ones (preservation of territorial integrity and sovereignty and security to the life and property of the people) and security issues of a State are not static. The priority on the types of national interests and security issues depends on the prevailing circumstances and the relative capabilities of the State. The security policy of a State protects and promotes national interests by neutralizing or defeating the security challenges. Now, India's core national interests are

i. preservation of territorial integrity and national sovereignty;
ii. ensuring the life and people at home and abroad;
iii. maintaining status quo in South Asia,
iv. securing greater international participation on issues of regional and global interests,
v. attaining permanent membership of the UN,
vi. building a multi-polar world with India as one of the many power centers,
vii. ensuring more democratization of the international institutions like the UN, WTO etc.

The following are the most vital security challenges that India now externally faces in its attempts to promote national interests:

i. *US's unilateralism in international affairs,*
ii. Western's interferences in the internal affairs of weaker states through justification of humanitarian intervention,
iii. International terrorism,
iv. Unresolved territorial disputes with neighbors particularly with China and Pakistan,

v. Continuation of Sino-Pakistani strategic cooperation,

vi. Problems like militancy and insurgency, refugee and illegal migration from across the border.

Security Policy

There is a continuing debate about how India should response to the security challenges and meets its national interests. Like political realism, one school of thought strongly holds the view that military capability continues to maintain its influence in achieving security goals. As a result, they argue that India's national interests would be in jeopardy if it does not maintains substantial military power with minimum nuclear strike capability against the potential nuclear adversaries.[27] Therefore, this school of thought strongly emphasizes on military modernization program- both conventional and non-conventional. The school now dominates India's security policymaking. India's continuous researches in indigenous ballistic missile development program and strategic cooperation with Russia and even with Israel[28] are good evidences in this regard. However, unlike the realists, the proponents of this school assume that the concept of security is interdependent and this is especially relevant in South Asian context. India always perceives China's as a 'transnational' power and its determination to expand its influence in South Asia as threat to its status quo. Similarly, Pakistan's intractable quest for parity with India aims at countering India's growing influence in South Asia. This created a triangular strategic competition involving three nuclear powers in the region.[29] India's Chinese threat perception will continue to persist if Chinese military modernization program and its strategic linkage with Pakistan continue. This urges India to carry on a minimum military preparedness program against any possible Chinese military strike. On the other hand, given historical animosity between Pakistan and India, Pakistan considers such a move of India as threat to its security.

We need to ask two vital questions here. Can military power alone help India in overcoming its security problems? In other words, how long can India sustain its defense preparedness program without or with low economic prosperity?

From the experiences, it seems that military power is not always a viable force in containing or solving problems like militancy/insurgency, refugee and illegal trans-border movement (migration) of people. India deployed thousands of military and para-military forces in Jammu and Kashmir and North East India to contain or crush down militancy/insurgency. However, solution of these problems is still far cry. Similarly, security forces failed to contain illegal trans-border movement of people. This has fuelled communal tension between the natives and migrants and created societal insecurity in many of the North-Eastern Indian states, particularly in Assam, Tripura and Maghalaya: Many feel that an integrative regional security dialogue shall be an effective strategy in tackling these problems and ameliorating the social security of the peoples of South Asia.[30] India's military might with a minimum nuclear deterrence may deter China from taking another military adventurism like the 1962 one or forcefully imposing an unacceptable military solution of the unresolved border problem. It may also help India overcoming the apprehension of Western humanitarian intervention or imposing an unbalanced Western mediation over the Kashmir problem. However, in true sense, it never creates durable security stability or peaceful environment in South Asia. Misperception and miscalculation between India and China and more particularly between India and Pakistan may bring an immediate danger of nuclear catastrophe. Here many argue that better relations with China shall improve India's security environment in South Asia largely. It will help not only in checkmating Sino-Pakistani strategic nexus, but it also helps India in troop's deployment in large number to the Indo-Pakistani border in case of security urgency. They believe, a speedy solution of the unresolved territorial dispute with some flexibility shall remarkably improve and broaden Sino-India relations in diverse areas including the security sector.[31]

However, the immediate threat of nuclear brinkmanship emanates not from Sino-Indian love and hated relations, but from the much-strained India-Pakistan relations. That is why, another group of scholars argue, so long as China, India and Pakistan cannot overcome the present security and diplomatic orthodoxies, the hope for durable stability and peace in South Asia is less likely. For meeting this noble objective, they argue, Beijing, New Delhi and Islamabad must undertake a series of bi-lateral and trilateral initiatives, both political and arms control.[32]

A long-term military potential highly depends on the strength and stability of the economic infrastructure and internal security (political stability).[33] In other words, for sustainability of the military infrastructural development program, India needs to enjoy stability in its economic growth rate. Many believe that India can significantly overcome this problem by building a harmonized society through the promotion of democratic values and spread of communitarian ideals and containing its internal problems like politics of criminalization and communalization.

Conclusion

From the above discussion, it is clear that a paradigm shift in national and international security study is yet to occur. Nation states are still embroiled with the traditional security ambiguity. The continuous enhancement of military strike capability (conventional and nuclear) by nuclear and nuclear threshold and non-nuclear weaponized states, the US's plan to militarize the space (NMD) and stiff opposition of China and Russia to such plan reflect that nation states are still embroiled with the traditional security approach. The recent US's led Iraq war without the UN sanction seriously questioned the creditability of this globally represented international institution in imposing its order on the nation states.

A paradigm shift in the international security study requires ratification and implementation of arms control and arms reduction treaties like START-I, START-II, NPT, CTBT Chemical and Biological Convention. The nuclear weaponized States (both declared and threshold) also need unconditional reduction and elimination of nukes. Similarly, the WTO also requires more institutionalization and democratization. However, such an outcome is very least likely because the powerful States are not co-operative in this regard. The provision of computer simulation tests under the CTBT (a monopoly of the N-5) is a clear indication in this regard.

This is however not to say that there is absence of institutionalized form of cooperation. Nevertheless, as John Mearsheimer argues, the incompatibility of state's goals and interests in the era of globalization enhances the competitive nature in the anarchic system and makes conflict as inevitable as cooperation.[34]

In India, we find, while there is a dominant feeling about the military role in achieving goals of national interests, many believe that India needs to witness economic prosperity to overcome its internal security exigencies by promoting its institutional values and spreading communitarian ideals. However, the thesis argues that security to be comprehensive requires not only economic prosperity and a strong military might but also 'good governance.'[35] A Nation's security is never comprehensive if one region faces the problems of unabated insurgency and illegal migration. That is, the concept of national security should not mean only for the majority communities, but also include the interests of the minority communities living within the national boundary. Therefore, national security is defined here from both the external and internal perspectives. In other words, national security should mean as a concept, which helps the state in not only maintaining its territorial integrity and independent identity in external environment, but also in preserving its core values and protecting the lives and properties of its citizens through good governance in the internal atmosphere. The CHT political crisis of Bangladesh is not an immediate military threat to national security of India. However, as the process of islimization continues in the CHT with more settlement of Muslims, it may pose a serious threat to not only its values of democracy, but also its economic and geo-strategic interests in the end.

NOTES AND REFERENCES

1. Manobendra Narayan Larma, the founder of the PCJSS used first the term 'Jumma' in the 1970s to present a separate collective identification of the thirteen ethnic groups of the CHT from the Bengali community. Before 1970s, they were called by themselves as 'hill people' because they mostly lived in the hilly areas. The Government of Bangladesh calls them as 'tribal people'. Therefore, throughout the thesis, the terms 'hill people', Jumma people and tribal people have used interchangeably. The term 'Jumma' has been derived from 'Jum' a kind of cultivation, (also known as slash and burn cultivation/shifting cultivation), which is generally practiced on the slopes of hilly areas. All these ethnic groups of the CHT once used to depend on this type of cultivation for their livelihood.
2. For instance, Sneha Kumar Chakma, Ganasyam Dewan, Lalit Mohan Chakma, the contemporary leaders of these ethnic groups wanted merger of the CHT with the Union of India and for the purpose, they met several times the contemporary national leaders of India. For details see Subir Bhaumik, "Strategic Pawn: India's Policy in the CHT", in Subir Bhaumik et.al. *Living on the Edge: Essays on the Chittagong Hill Tracts*,. Kathmandu: South Asia Forum for Human Rights, 1997, p. 140. Similar opinion had also been reflected in a memorandum, which laid down the political demands of the CHT's people to the committee of India's Constituent Assembly. The Chittagong Hill Tracts Peoples Association (CHTPA) submitted it on February 15, 1997. Also, *see the letter of the CHTPA to Dr. Syamaprasad Mukerjee,* which expressed displeasure and disappointment over the Government of India's intransigent response for the CHT's merger with Union of India, 24 January 1948.
3. For instance, Chakma, Tripura, Mog (Marma), Lushai,

Bhowm live in large number in Mizoram and Tripura states of India. The partition of the Indian sub-continent divided these communities and now they live on both sides of the international border.

4. The Parbattya Chattagram Jana Samhati Samiti (PCJSS) was formed in the post liberation period of Bangladesh. The primary objective of this party was to fight for the rights of the Jummas of the CHT in the post independent period of Bangladesh. After prolonged fighting against Bangladesh security establishment, it finally laid down arms on 2 December 1997, when it signed a peace accord with the Government of Bangladesh.
5. The United Peoples Democratic Front (UPDF) was formed on 26 December 1998 by the members of a faction of once three frontline democratic organizations of the PCJSS-- Hill Students Council (HSC), Hill Peoples Council (HPC) and Hill Women Federation (HWF). This party expressed dissatisfaction over the contents of the peace accord and vowed to fight for full autonomy for the Jumma people. For details, see the Primary Declaration of the UPDF, 26 December 1998, and http//: www.updfcht.org, the official website of the UPDF.
6. Jayantanuja Bandyopadhyaya, *The Making of India's Foreign Policy,* Calcutta: Allied Publishers, 1991, p. 10.
7. See John Baylis, "International and global security in the post cold-war", in John Baylis et. al., *The Globalization of World's Politics,* Oxford: Oxford University Press, 2001, p. 255.
8. Bandhyopadhyaya, *op. cit.*, pp. 9-10,
9. Baylis, *op.cit.*, p .255.
10. For non-military threat to security, see the introductory and concluding chapters of P.R. Chari (ed), *Perspective on National Security in South Asia: In Search of a New Paradigm,* New Delhi: Manohar, 2000. The concept of comprehensive security developed by Delhi Policy Group also identifies the non-military threat to the security of a nation. For details on 'comprehensive security', see, Lt. General (Rtd.) V.R. Raghvan, *Comprehensive Security*; a Field Marshal Cariappa Memorial Lecture, New Delhi, 7 October 2001.
11. See for instance, Jack Donnelly, *Realism and International Relations*, Cambridge: Cambridge University Press, 2000, pp.16-17, Arthur A. Stein, *Why Nations Cooperate,* Ithaca: Cornel University Press, 1990, pp. 4-5.
12. Morghenthau as quoted in Jack Donnelly, op. cit. p. 46. Also,

see, Arthur A. Stein, *Why Nations Cooperate*, Ithaca: Cornel University Press, 1990. Hans. J. Morghenthau, *Politics among Nations*, New Delhi: Kalyani Publishers, 1985, pp. 4-5 & 53-57.

13. Baylis, *op. cit.*, p.247.
14. Jack Donnelly, *op. cit.*, p. 17.
15. Jack Donnelly, *op. cit.*, p. 17
16. *Ibid.*
17. Steve L. Lamy, "Contemporary Mainstream Approaches: Neo-realism and Neo-Liberalism", in John Baylis et. al, *op.cit.*, p. 187. Also for detailed analysis about the prisoner's dilemm game' in international relations and cooperation among the nation states that is arisen out of the dilemmas of common interests and common aversions, see Stein, *op. cit.*, pp. 32-42.
18. Lamy, *op. cit.*, p.191, Donnelly, *op.cit.*, p. 29.
19. Baylis, *op.cit.*, pp. 262-63.
20. Lamy, *op.cit.*, p. 194.
21. For detailed analysis, see Mark Ritchie et.al., *WTO and the Globalization of Food Insecurity*, San Francisco: International Forum on Globalization (IFG), 1999, pp.13-27, Vandana Shiva, "War against Nature and the People of the South", in Surah Anderson (ed.), *View From The South: The Effect of Globalization and the WTO on The Third World Countries*, San Francisco: IFG, c,d, pp. 144-116, Martin Khor, "Development Trade and Environment: Third World Perspective" in Vandana Shiva et.al., *The Future of Progress: Reflection on Environment and Development*, Dehradun : Natraj, 1994, p.41-42 and Mustapha Kamal Pasha, "Globalization and Poverty in South Asia", *Millennium*, vol. 25, No. 3, 1996, pp. 642-50.
22. Paul Hirst, *War and Power in the 21st Century*, Cambridge: Polity Press, 2001, p. 122.
23. For detailed analysis about "regime formation and regime change, see Stein, *op.cit.*, pp. 50-53.
24. Baylis, *op. cit.*, p. 266.
25. *Ibid.*, pp. 267-68.
26. *Ibid.*, pp. 265-66.
27. For instance, see Raju G.C. Thomas, "India's Security Environment", in P. Sahadevan (ed.), *Conflict and Peacemaking in South Asia*, New Delhi: Lancer's Book, 2001, pp. 78-79. Parvin Sawhney, an expert on Strategic Studies opines that the Prime Minister Rajiv Gandhi's historical visit to China in 1988 became possible because of India's development of a credible military force against China. For detail, see Parvin Sawhney, "India, China and Pakistan: Conventional Military

Rivalry", in the same book, pp. 108, 160-162.

28. India was a staunch supporter to the Palestinian liberation movement. Moreover, having a large size of Muslim population and firm ideological commitment against colonialism, India was not persuaded in establishing full fledged diplomatic relations with Israel until 1997 when the then Israel's President Mr. Ezer Weizemen paid a week long official visit to New Delhi. Since then, India entered into numerous military deals with Israel. The proposed sale of Phalcons, known as AWACS to India is the latest one.
29. P. Sahadevan, "Competing Regional Interests, Conflicts Formation and Conflict Management in South Asia" in P. Sahadevan (ed.), *Conflict and Peace Making in South Asia, op. cit.*, pp. 20-26.
30. Ross Mallick, *Ethnicity and Human Rights in South Asia*, New Delhi: Sage Publication, 1998, pp. 8-37. Crumbling of democratic institutions, alienation of minority population (political and religious persecution and economic deprivation), nexus between corrupt elements in the governing apparatus are the three most important factors that led generation of ethnic insurgency, refugee problem and illegal trans-border movement of people in South Asia. Among the South Asian states, India has been more victimized to this problem than the other has. Refugees in large number from Bangladesh, Srilanka, Nepal, and Tibet have poured into India from time to time. Therefore, unless social, political and economic security of the people is not improved, this problem will continue to plague the South Asian security environment. For details see, P.R. Chari (eds.), *Perspectives on National Security in South Asia: In Search of a New Paradigm*, op. cit. and *Security and Governance in South Asia*, New Delhi: Manohar, 2001, pp.159-78.
31. C.V. Ranganathan and Vinod C. Khanna, *India and China: The Way Ahead After 'Mao's India War'*, New Delhi: Har Anand, 2000, pp. 155-81, Arun Kumar Banerji, "India-China Relations: Retrospect and Prospects" in Arun Kumar Banerji et. al., *Peoples Republic of China at Fifty*, New Delhi: Lancers' Book, 2001, pp. 32-50.
32. Kanti P. Bajpai, "Managing a Strategic Triangle: India, China and Pakistan" in P. Sahadevan (ed.), *"Conflict and Peace Making in South Asia"*, op. cit, pp. 84-103, Swaran Singh, "Controlling Interstate Competition through CBMs", in the same book, pp. 164-83.

33. Bandyopadhyaya, *op.cit.*, p. 11.
34. For John Mearsheimer on the possibility of cooperation among the nation states in the era of globalization, see Baylis, *op.cit.*, p. 267.
35. Good governance includes the following features: i. Promotion of efficiency and transparency in public administration, ii. Respect for human rights and rule of law, iii. Greater role for the civilian bodies in monitoring and managing the security sector. For details about good governance, see P.R. Chari, "Security and Governance in South Asia: Their Linkages", in P.R. Chari, (ed.), *Security and Governance in South Asia*, op. cit. p. 14.

2

The Chittagong Hill Tracts Political Crisis and Political Movement of the Jummas

After prolonged negotiations, the PCJSS and the Government of Bangladesh (GoB) signed a peace accord. The objective was to establish peace and political stability in the CHT. However, as seen in the introduction, several factors like political antagonism with armed confrontation between the PCJSS and the UPDF, non-implementation of the peace accord by the Government of Bangladesh (GoB) made the post accord political environment of the CHT more complicated and volatile. The UPDF and the PCJSS are not different in ideological orientation. Their political goals are also same. However, despite having same political objectives and ideological orientation, why are they fighting against each other? Why did the GoB fail to implement the peace accord?

Before addressing these fundamental questions, we need to understand the nature of the CHT political crisis and political movement of the Jummas. This chapter in its first section analyzes the background of the CHT political crisis and the role of the political factors, which have been responsible for prolonging the CHT political crisis. The second section deals with the nature of the political movement of the Jummas. While analyzing this, it would argue that the political movement of the Jummas has never attained the status of separatism. The following section looks at the post accord political administration of the CHT and analyzes it in term of good governance. The conclusion would attempt to analyze the reasons for political instability of the CHT in the post accord situation with reference to the analysis of the above sections in general and the third section in particular.

I

BACKGROUND OF THE CHT POLITICAL CRISIS: CAUSES FOR CONTINUATION OF THE PROBLEM

According to Mr. Mukut Khanti Khisa[1]

> Historically the Jummas are victims of the British colonial disengagement policy from the Indian sub-continent. Had the British awarded the CHT into the Union of India taking into consideration the interests and opinion of the Jummas and in the spirit of the Two-Nation Theory, they would not have been politically suffered and victimized much.

Most of the Jumma politicians and social workers share Mr. Khisa's opinion.[2] They argue that the CHT political crisis is a legacy of the British colonial disengagement policy. Naturally, the question arises-how and where did the British Indian administration make its mistake while deciding on the political future of the CHT during partition of the Indian sun-continent?

The British colonial disengagement policy in the Indian sub-continent created two self-governing dominions-India and Pakistan. While Pakistan was formed with amalgamation of the Muslim majority populated states and districts, India was created with integration of the non-Muslim populated states and districts. Now let us look at the composition of the CHT's population during partition:

Composition of Muslim and non-Muslim population in the CHT in 1947:[3]

Total population	247,053
Non-Muslim population-	239, 783 viz. 97.06% of the total population
Muslim population	7,270 viz. 2.94% of the total population

It is clear that non-Muslim population consisted 97.06% of the total CHT's population during the time of partition. Therefore, the principles of Two-Nation Theory justified natural merger of the CHT with the Union of India. However, much against the wishes of the Jummas, Sir Cyril Radcliff, the chairperson of the Bengal Boundary Commission declared integration of the CHT with Pakistan on 16th August 1947. The Radcliff Commission argued that CHT was geographically isolated from the majority non-Muslim areas of Bengal. Moreover, there was a historical economic dependency between the people of the CHT and the Chittagong port. Therefore, circumstances demanded integration of the CHT with Pakistan (East Pakistan). Lord Mountbatten also observed the economic relations between the people of the CHT and the Chittagong port and he explained it in the following words: [4]

> ...the complete economic life of the people of the CHT depends upon East Bengal... There are only one or two different tracts through the jungle in Assam and it would be disastrous for the people themselves... In a sense Chittagong, the only port of East Bengal also depends upon the CHT.

Nevertheless, the Commission's decision to integrate the CHT with Pakistan on the basis of the above observations was unjustified and even unconstitutional on many grounds:

First, Historically, the CHT was never under Bengal's administration. The Chakma Chiefs fought several times against the Muslim and British rulers for maintaining autonomy in the CHT's administration. For instance, Chakma Chief Jalllal Kha fought a war in 1714 against the Muslim Nawab of Bengal. In 1777 and 1781, Chakma Chief Sher Dalot Kha fought twice against the English East India Company and glorified victory in it. It was only Jan Bashk Kha, the later Chakma Chief accepted the British suzereignty when the Company imposed economic blockade against the hill people. Therefore, acknowledging the fighting spirit and reluctance of the Chakma Chiefs to be British's subjects, Mr. Hulked, the British Commissioner of the Chittagong said in 1829:[5]

> ... The hill tribes of Chittagong were not British subjects, but merely tributaries and that he recognized no right of the British to interfere with internal arrangements.

Consequently, the British administration felt from time to time the necessity of preserving autonomy of the hill people until its departure from the Indian sub-continent.

Moreover, as the CHT was not under the direct administration of Bengal, it did not have any representation in Bengal's legislature. When the Governor of Bengal brought the CHT within its administrative jurisdiction, the contemporary Chakma Chief opposed it and decided to remain outside the Provincial Ministry's administration. Hence, the Bengal Boundary Commission, which was formed based on deliberations of the members of the Bengal's legislature, did not have any legal jurisdiction to decide on the CHT's political future.

Secondly, Shylet, a Muslim majority populated district of Assam had merged with East Pakistan through a referendum. Since the CHT's people also wanted its (CHT) merger with India, the British Indian administration could have arranged a similar referendum to decide on the political future of the CHT, considering it even as an ordinary district of Bengal.

Thirdly, although it was geographically isolated from the non-Muslim populated areas of Bengal, it had geographical proximity with Tripura and Mizoram (then a part of Assam). Like the CHT's the lines of communication in the Northeast were also not developed during partition. Therefore, if economically, the CHT's people were dependent on the Chittagong port, so were the people of Tripura and lower parts of Assam (Mizoram, Megalaya).

The Bengal Boundary Commission overlooked all these facts. As stated earlier, most of the Jumma politicians and social workers strongly hold the views that following the spirit of the Two Nation Theory, had the CHT been integrated with secular democratic India, they would have been economically and culturally much developed. Although their argument seems to be value laded, yet it has empirical reality. Whereas, they are now struggling for political autonomy in Bangladesh, the CHT, by now, they would have a separate state with a legislature within India. Therefore, they would have political representation in both the state and the Union legislatures. However, the present conditions of the Jummas (particularly the Chakmas) are very pathetic. The Chakmas are still struggling for political rights in Arunachal Pradesh. They still face the threat of eviction from there. The Chakmas of Mizoram have an Autonomous District Council (formed in 1971 under the Sixth Schedule of the Indian constitution). However, they also face the problem of eviction and disenfranchisement.[6] In Assam the Chakmas, who are mostly concentrated in the Karbianglong and Cacher districts, are politically and economically the most marginalized and disadvantaged and remain under occasional threat of eviction from the Karbi national army (a Karbi based insurgent group active particularly in these two districts of Assam). In Tripura, they are victims in the politics of communalism. The Bengalis develop suspicion towards the Chakmas for their racial similarity and cultural proximity with the greater tribal society in the state. On the other hand, Tripuri (Debberma, Jamatia, and Reang) based insurgent outfits- All Tripura Tiger Force (ATTF), National Liberation Front of Tripura (NLFT) and tribal but primarily Tripuri based local political party- Indigenous Peoples Front of Tripura (INPT)[7] are skeptical towards the Chakmas. They find a closer political proximity between the Chakmas and the Bengalis because like the Bengalis, many Chakmas have been migrated to the state from East Pakistan.[8] In the CHT of Bangladesh, their conditions are more deplorable than Indian Chakmas (discussed in the later part of this chapter).

There are several factors, which are responsible for escalation and continuation of the CHT political crisis:

I. Dissolution of the special status provision of the CHT and construction of Kaptai dam

The Pakistani Muslim League (PML) from the beginning developed suspicion towards the Jummas (particularly the Chakmas) for their pro-Indian leaning and pro-Indian agitation during partition. Naturally, it was deterministic to annihilate them in post independent politics of Pakistan. An East Pakistani Muslim League member therefore expressed.[9]

> "If necessary we shall tame the tribal like elephants."

The first move of the Pakistani Muslim League to annihilate the Jummas was its attempt to include the CHT with the province of East Bengal (East Pakistan) as an ordinary district in 1955. However, the move was failed. Colonel Niblett, the last British born Deputy Commissioner of the CHT and the Chakma chief strongly opposed the decision. However, the PML did not stop there. In 1963, the Pakistani regime abolished the special status provision of the CHT by constitutional amendment. It amended Rule 51 of the CHT Manual[10], Rule 54 [11] and Rule 34[12]. All these steps empowered the non-hill people with the right to residence and the right to have property by virtue of their continuous stay of 15 years in the CHT. It suffices to say that the process of political alienation of the hill people began within the state of Pakistan.

Pakistan constructed a large hydroelectric project on the Karnafuli River at Rangamati life. It destroyed the economic backbone of the hill people beyond reparation between 1957 and 1962. The project benefited the Bengalis in many ways.[13] However; it brought devastating consequences for the hill people. The dam inundated an area of about 400 sq. miles including 5400 acres of cultivable land making up to 40% of the CHT's total land acreage. It displaced and made homeless near about 10, 0000 persons (mostly Chakmas). Their leaders alleged that the Government did not provide adequate rehabilitation and compensation package to the victims.[14]

The dissolution of the CHT special political status by the 1963 constitutional amendment was a big blow to the political life of the hill people. Similarly, the construction of the Kaptai dam without their concern and participation and adequate rehabilitation and compensation program was a big blow to their economic.

II. Political and economic marginalization of the Jummas in the politics of Bangladesh

The following factors are mainly responsible for political and economic marginalization of the Jummas in the post independent politics of Bangladesh:

Racial discrimination policy of the Government of Bangladesh

Internationally all the consecutive GoBs stood against all forms of racial discrimination. Bangladesh. They condemned minority racist regime of South Africa and maintained no diplomatic, political, economic or cultural link with it. The GoBs also opposed the settlement of the Jews settlers in the occupied Arab territories, sponsored many resolutions like resolution NO 1992/2A and 2B at the 38th session of the UN on human rights in 1992.[15] It does not have yet any diplomatic relations with Israel because of its alleged racial discrimination policy against the Palestinian people.

However, in national politics, all the successive regimes of Bangladesh discriminated the hill people of the CHT and other 'indigenous people[16] of Bangladesh on racial ground through systemic reign of terror, force confiscation of properties, religious and political persecution in total contravention to its international commitment against racism. The founder of Bangladesh and icon of the Bangladesh liberation movement Sheikh Mujibur Rahman was himself a racist against the hill people. The racist orientation in his political philosophy against the Jummas had been reflected in many of his political decisions. For example, Mr. Rahman during the course of Parliamentary debate in 1972 said:[17]

> "Our ideology is clear. This ideology has inspired us to attain independence and this ideology shall constitute the basis of this state. Nationalism – Bengali Nationalism shall be the main pillar of this state. Bengali nationalism encompasses Bengali culture, Bengali heritage..."

Similarly, in an electoral speech at Rangamati in 1973, he advised the *Jummas (without any hesitation) to be Bengalis by heart*.[18]

Mr. Rahman rejected the cultural assimilation theory of nation's formation within the politics of Pakistan. He vehemently opposed cultural imposition of the West Pakistanis on the Bengalis and sought for recognition of Bengali to be the official language of East Pakistan. However, in the post independent politics of Bangladesh, it was he, who first adopted this assimilationist tradition of nation building, albeit Bangladesh is a multi cultural and multinational state. Consequently, the constitution of independent Bangladesh revealed dominant bias for the Bengali community. It failed largely to incorporate and protect the interests of the hill people and other indigenous peoples at the time of its framing. Therefore, the 1972 constitution of Bangladesh did not recognize the existence of other national minority communities. Article 3 of Part I recognized Bengali as the State language and Article 6 of Part I declared all citizens of Bangladesh as Bengalis.[19]

Sheikh Mujibur Rahman was assassinated in 1975. Therefore, he did get enough time to implement his policies. Nevertheless, all the consecutive GoBs attempted to materialize his racist ideology in various ways. This racist policy encouraged political implantation of Muslim Bengali settlers into the CHT from other parts of Bangladesh. Being racist in nature, the population implantation policy created communal tension between the Jummas and the politically implanted settlers. Moreover, as it has heinous political orientation, the civil military administration overtly and covertly backed the settlers in their coercive operations against the Jummas.[20]

Militarization of the CHT

Sheikh Mujib's Bangladesh considered the autonomy movement of the Jummas as a secessionist movement. Therefore, he took it as a threat to national security of Bangladesh. Naturally, Bangladesh in Sheikh Mujib's era per se felt the importance of militarization of the CHT. As a consequence, within less than five years (i.e. 1971-1975), three military cantonments were set up in Dighinala, Ruma and Alikadam and an Ansar (para-military) battalion at Gangra.[21] The GoB also established four Brigade Headquarters in 1975 in Rangamati, Khagrachari and Dighinala and Bandarban. Besides these, the GoB deployed another nineteen infantry battalions, eleven Bangladesh Riffle (BDR) battalions, three artillery battalions, one engineer battalion, eighteen Ansar battalions and four battalion of armed force in different parts of the CHT.[22] It established a naval base at the Kaptai Lake consisting three gunboats.[23] The CHT Commission, which visited the CHT in 1990 reported that full-scale militarization in the CHT had created a military-civilian (Jumma) ratio-1:13.[24]

What are factors that led to full-scale militarization of the CHT in the post Mujib's era? Several factors played significant role behind full-scale militarization of the CHT in the post Mujib Bangladesh. In the first place, Sheihk Mujib himself wanted militarization of the CHT. The post Mujib Bangladesh just wanted to carry that on. Secondly, military assumed central role in the decision-making process. It led to marginalization of the civilian institutions. Thirdly, bilateral relations between India and Bangladesh deteriorated severely. The PCJSS also intensified the movement then. The military government in Bangladesh developed suspicion towards India for its alleged covert involvement in the CHT affairs. Fourthly, the PCJSS formed its armed wing- Shanti Bahini (SB, meaning peace force) and began military operations against the security forces of Bangladesh in the CHT. The GoB, in its immediate reaction against such development decided to outlaw PCJSS and felt the importance of militarization of the whole region. Finally, like Mujib, the military administration also viewed the autonomy movement of the hill people as secessionist movement and perceived it as a threat to territorial and political integration of Bangladesh.

Militarization of the CHT, formation of SB by the PCJSS, military operations by the SB and counter insurgency operation of the security forces of Bangladesh caused not only severe break down in the law and order situation with regular human rights violations, but it also increased enmity between the Jummas and the Bengali (Muslim) community in the CHT.

Implantation of Settlers into the CHT from Plain Districts

Article 36 of the Bangladesh's constitution states that 'subject to any reasonable restrictions imposed by law in the public interests, every citizen shall have the right to move freely throughout Bangladesh, to reside and settle in place therein and to leave and re-enter Bangladesh'. Similarly, Article 42(1) provides that 'subject to any restrictions imposed by law, every citizen has the right to acquire, hold, transfer or otherwise depose of property ....'[25]

However, the constitution did not specify what these reasonable restrictions are and when and where to impose these restrictions. Article 19 of the Indian constitution also provides similar rights to the citizens of India. However, it clearly states that these reasonable restrictions are imposed when the interests of the Schedule Tribes are involved. For example, freedom of residence in any part of India is a fundamental right for every citizen of India. Yet restrictions have been imposed on the Indian citizens visiting tribal majority states like the Arunachal Pradesh, Mizoram, and Sikim. Indians other than permanent residents of these states have to procure 'inner line permit' for visiting these states.[26] Taking the advantage of absence of a well-defined legal interpretation of these two articles, the GoB justified population transfer from plain districts into the CHT. As a result, the GoB between

1979 and 1984 settled approximately 200000 to 400000 landless Bengali settlers in the CHT. The government assured providing per family with 5 acres of hilly lands, 4 acres of mixed lands and 2.5 acres of paddy lands.[27] However, it would appear that implantation of Bengali settlers had more political motivation than providing economic security to the settlers in the CHT. Because, in the first place, the Government used the settlers as human shield for the security forces against the military operations of the SB.[28] Therefore, the Government initially rehabilitated these settlers near the military camps and outposts. Secondly, the settlement process was aimed at reducing the percentage of the hill people in the CHT. The GoB achieved this objective. According to the Bangladesh's population census report of 1991, the percentage of the hill people population reached at 51%. Besides, as there had been no restriction for further settlement of Bengalis, it is popularly believed that within the last one and half decade, thousands have been unofficially settled thereby converting them into further minority.[29] Thirdly, it created tremendous land pressure (particularly plain and paddy lands) in the CHT. In 1964, the Forestall and Engineering International Ltd., a Canadian company in a study on the CHT's soils and topography stated that only 33% of the CHT's lands were suitable for agriculture, and 77% for a forestation. Now, at an average, if a family consists of 5 members (informal calculation), [30] the lands required for the total members of settlers' families:

(a) Minimum estimate of 40,000 families (200,000÷5)

(b) Minimum estimate of 80,000 families (400,000÷5)

Acres of land required	*Minimum (a)*	*Maximum (b)*
Paddy land	40,000 x 2.5 = 100,000	80,000 x 2.5 = 200,000
Mixed land	40,000 x 4.0 = 160,000	80,000 x 4.0 = 320,000
Hilly land	40,000 x 5.0 = 200,000	80,000 x 5.0 = 400,000
Total (in acres)	460,000	920,000

As per the gradation of lands in the CHT, only 104,304.64 acres (as the report of the Canadian Forestall Company stated) of paddy lands are available. However, for settling an estimated 80,000 settler families with 2.5 acres of paddy land (as per the GoB's assurance to the settlers), the CHT alone requires 200,000 acres of paddy lands. The policy of population transfer created severe land pressure in the CHT. Since it has pre-planned political objective, therefore, most of the settlers have been rehabilitated in the valleys nearby the cultivable fields. It is also necessary to mention here that there are also many flaws in the traditional land laws of the hill people.[31] The civil-military administration in the CHT took this advantage and encouraged the settlers to encroach and grab lands of the Jummas. This created communal tensions and ethnic strife between Jummas and the Bengali settlers. Such an ugly political environment displaced thousands of Jummas in different parts of the CHT in general and Feni, Matiranga, Guimara, Betbonia etc. particular.

Lack of National Political Consensus to deal with the CHT Problem

The CHT political crisis is a national problem of

Bangladesh.[32] But the major political parties – the Awami League (AL), the Bangladesh Nationalist Party (BNP), Jatiyo Party –Ershad (JP-E) and Jamati Islami (JI) could never reach at a national political consensus in framing up common agenda to deal with the CHT political crisis. The first three of the above stated political parties entered into a series of political dialogue with the PCJSS for political settlement of the problem. General Hossain Mohammad Ershad formed three Hill District Local Government Councils in 1989 in three districts of the CHT. A faction of the PCJSS surrendered following it. However, the other political parties did not endorse General Ershad's decision. The BNP led GoB and the PCJSS also concluded several rounds of peace talks between 1992 and 1995, but they failed to reach at a settlement. Later on, the AL government and the PCJSS singed a peace agreement on 2nd December 1997 after protracted negotiations. But, other three political parties did not welcome it. Instead, they vehemently criticized the AL and denounced the accord by branding it anti-national, unconstitutional and total sell out of the country's territory to India. How far is this allegation right?

The contents of the peace-accord and its national and international legal validity show that their allegation is baseless. It did not have any constitutional validity because the accord was not concluded by any constitutional amendment. There was also no third party's mediation to motor the implementation process of the peace accord. (See the later part of this section). Now the question is--if their allegation was groundless, then why did they oppose the peace-accord?

Before analyzing this question, we need to look at the factors that restrained the BNP and AL from extending political support to General Ershad's peace process with the PCJSS. In the first place, General Ershad was a military dictator. He imposed a ruthless military rule throughout the country. Towards the end of 1980s, there was popular opposition against military rule. The movement for restoration and reinstallation of democratic institutions was highly intensified. Therefore, the AL and BNP were convinced that military dictator's possible success in a popular settlement of the CHT political crisis could become a political weapon in strengthening and consolidating his position, which would mean further extension of military rule in the country. Secondly, General Ershad did not seriously seek political support and co-operation from these two influential political parties. Therefore, he ignored their political interests involved in a possible settlement of the problem.

On the other hand, BNP, JP-E and JI opposed the 1997's peace-accord mainly for the following reasons: The AL politicized the CHT peace peace-accord. Although the JP-E and BNP had contributions to the peace-process, like general Ershad, the AL also did not recognize their contributions. Instead, the AL blamed the military ruler and the BNP for their intransigent and non-flexible attitudes towards the hill people. It argues that the BNP and JP-E lacked sincerity and political will to deal with the problem. In this way, the AL took every credit for its success in reaching at a political settlement with the PCJSS. The AL's supporters displayed posters and banners throughout Bangladesh, which read: *"Sheikh Hasinar Abodan, Parbatty Chattogram Samachar Samadan."*[33] (The solution of the CHT political crisis is a great contribution and success of Sheikh Hasina). Secondly, there are many,[34] who maintain that the main reason behind the BNP's opposition to the pace-accord was that it also wanted to reach at a negotiated settlement with the PCJSS by concluding a peace-accord of 1997 type. However, it could not reach at such settlement due to the alleged PCJSS's non-flexible stand on its political demands. Thirdly, JI opposed the peace-accord because it believed that the accord did not address the concerns of the Muslim Bengalis living in the CHT in many respects.[35]

Implementation of the CHT peace-accord is now at hang due to absence of political consensus among the major political parties of Bangladesh. The AL did not implement the accord looking at the intensity of popular opposition garnered by the BNP, JP-E and JI and keeping in mind the party's prospects in the General Election of 2001. The BNP led coalition government did not have any sincerity and commitment towards the implementation peace accord.[36]

Division in Jumma Leadership

The Jumma leadership did not also have unity in their struggle for autonomy for the Jumma people. The ideological rift among the top leaders of the PCJSS arising out the controversy between communism versus nationalism caused a bloody civil war in early 1980s. It divided the cadres into two groups. Until the outbreak of the civil war, SB carried on its military operations against the Bangladesh's security forces with high level of efficiency.[37] However, the civil war of

1980's demoralized many members of the SB and weakened the party largely. On the other, the Bangladesh's security forces exploited this situation in consolidating their strategic position throughout the CHT.

In the post accord situation, peace-accord, the Jumma people have been facing another bloody civil war between the PCJSS and the UDPF. Already hundreds have been killed in such violent armed clashes between the two groups.[38] Kidnapping the targeted individuals and extortion by the armed cadres of both groups are now happening throughout the CHT every now and then. This deteriorated seriously the law and order situation in the CHT.

II

POLITICAL MOVEMENT OF THE JUMMAS: AUTONOMY OR SEPARATISM

There are many within the Bangladesh's intellectual community who consider the political movement of the Jummas as separatist movement. They always use the term 'separatism, secessionism' while writing or presenting lectures on the CHT political crisis in national and international seminars, conferences etc.[39] The Jumma national leadership also frequently used the term 'self-determination' while fighting for the rights of the Jumma people. What is self-determination?

'Self-determination' had been generally explained in term of separatism. Lenin's theory of self-determination became popular in many radical movements during the 20th century. According to Lenin, self-determination of nations meant political separation and formation of independent nation-states.[40] He argued that the quest for national self-determination arose primarily in response to intolerable state of oppression. The Tamil struggle in Sri Lanka is a classic example in this regard. Initially it was constitutional but later on it turned into an organizing armed resistance against the state power, when it failed to achieve its political goals in constitutional way.

According to the Tamil Tigers,

> "the struggle for national freedom, having failed in its democratic popular agitations, having exhausted its moral power to mobilize the masses for peaceful campaigns, gave rise to armed resistance in Tamil Eelam.[41]

The Jumma national movement also developed through such an evolutionary process. Initially it began as a constitutional movement, but it transformed into an armed struggle in its attempt to form 'Jummaland'. Naturally question arises-did the Jumma national movement attained the character of separatism?

According to the Jumma political leadership, nationhood and statehood are two different concepts. Nationhood can be established even without being independent and sovereign. Paul R Brass, while writing on nations, nationalism and ethnicity also subscribed such an idea of nationhood. According to Brass, when an ethnic community aspires for a national status and recognition and succeeds in achieving these goals either within an existing state or in a state of its own, becomes a nation. In other, a nation is a particular type of ethnic community, which is politically organized with some recognized rights in a political system.[42] The PCJSS, first widely represented political party of the Jummas in post independent Bangladesh, maintained that Jumma nationhood could be constructed and established within the state of Bangladesh. Therefore, by the term, 'self-determination' the PCJSS meant the right to have national recognition of all the thirteen ethnic national minority groups of the CHT with political autonomy. The non-separatist nature of the CHT political movement can also be traced from the objectives behind the formation of the PCJSS. The PCJSS was formed in 1972 mainly with two important political objectives. The first one was to ensure the separate political status of the CHT with constitutional guarantee. The second was aimed at establishing regional autonomy with a legislative assembly.[43] This had further been reflected in 1972, when M.N. Larma, the founder of the PCJSS, submitted an 'appeal' before the Draft Framing Committee of the Constitution of Bangladesh requesting to pay due consideration to the following points while deciding on the status of the CHT:[44]

(i) The need to make the CHT a separate province with a democratic form of government,

(ii) The need to change the administrative pattern of the region with all the fundamental rights of the CHT peoples guaranteed,

(iii) The need for a constitutional status of the CHT that would ensure the 'national survival' of the tribal peoples of the area,

(iv) Administrative protection for all lands held by

the tribal-hills and slopes under 'Jhum' cultivation and institutional measures to prevent land alienation in the tribal areas,

(v) The need for institutional arrangements to prevent and deter settlements of plainsmen from other districts of the country in the CHT, so that the tribal could retain their demographic majority in the area.

The fundament demands of the PCJSS remained unchanged even after resorting to armed resistance against Bangladesh in the second half of 1970s. A part from restoration of traditional land rights and constitutional recognition of the Jummas, the PCJSS demanded demilitarization of the CHT, withdrawal of the politically implanted settlers and political autonomy with a separate legislature for the Jummas for an amicable political settlement of the problem.[45] The demands of the UPDF are also nothing new but a reiteration of the same demands as made by the PCJSS in the charter of the modified five point demands. The party in its *'Primary Declaration'* clearly stated that while fighting for the fundamental rights of the Jumma people; *it would respect sovereignty and territorial integrity of Bangladesh.*[46]

But the question is-- can the right to self-determination be enjoyed without politically being independent and sovereign?

According to Convention on Elimination of Racial Discrimination (CERD) committee, there are two aspects in the right of self-determination: internal and external. Internally, it means the rights of all peoples to pursue freely their economic, social and cultural development without outside interference. In other words, the government needs to represent the whole population without discrimination on the ground of race, color, descent or ethnic origin.47 On the other hand, the external dimension of self determination implies that all peoples have the right to determine freely their political status and their place in the international community on the basis of the principle of equal rights and exemplified by the liberation of peoples from colonialism and by the prohibition to subject peoples to alien subjugation, domination and exploitation.[48] According to Madam Erica-Irene A Daes,[49] the concept of self-determination has taken a new meaning in the postcolonial era. In her words,

> Once an independent state has been established and recognized, its constituent peoples must try to express their aspirations through the national political system, and not through creation of new states.[50]

It is clear that Madam Daes also holds the view that right of self determination can be enjoyed without creation of new states, when the existing state represent the aspirations of the whole population without any discrimination. However, Madam Daes argues, when the state fails to represent the wishes of all sections of the population, discriminate a section of population on racial and other grounds, secessionism can not be ruled out. It means that application of the external dimension of self determination arises only in response to state's belligerency against a section of a population. Therefore, self-determination can be interpreted in different ways. For instance, under the rule of military dictatorship, it can be interpreted as the right of peoples to elect their government in democratic order. While in democracy, it could mean as the right of the people at all levels to have a voice in the decisions, in which they are governed.

Maivan Clech Lam is another expert on self-determination in the postcolonial era. According to Lam, 'self-determination' and 'territorial integrity' are two different terms with two different legal dimensions. The concept of territorial integrity is related with the sovereignty of a state. Self-determination on the other hand is more related with creation of autonomous political institutions.[51] This connotation of self-determination is very significant especially for preservation and promotion of the indigenous peoples' rights. Because, for most of indigenous peoples, 'self-determination' means the right to freely pursue their economic, social and cultural development through self-government institutions within the framework of national unity and development. For instance, in Canada, the '*claims and settlement agreements*' between the state authorities and indigenous people, provided the indigenous people of Canada with similar institutional arrangement. In the Philippines, *the Indigenous Peoples Right Act of 1997* recognizes communal and individual rights of the indigenous peoples to their ancestral domain, ensures continued State's support for autonomy arrangements in the Cordilleras and Mindana. It also provides self-governance to them to pursue their economic, cultural and social development without questioning the Philippines' territorial integrity.[52]

It appears that the idea of self-determination can be established within the framework of a political system through institutional reforms. The Jumma people are also indigenous people because they fall within the legal framework of international definitions on indigenous peoples.[53] Therefore, they also demand similar institutional measures to protect and promote their distinct cultural heritages, values without questioning the sovereignty and territorial integrity of Bangladesh.

The political movement of the Jummas turned into an armed struggle in response to the state oppression within Bangladesh. Nevertheless, unlike the Tamil struggle in Sri Lanka, it did not attain the character of separatism. The concept of self-determination remained confined with the idea creation of autonomous political institutions within the political framework of Bangladesh.

III

POST ACCORD POLITICAL ADMINISTRATION IN THE CHT: AN EVALUATION IN TERM OF GOOD GOVERNANCE

The peace-agreement of 1997 between the PCJSS and the GoB led to the formation of the CHT Regional Council (CHTRC) in co-ordination with the three Hill District Councils of three districts of the CHT - Rangamati, Khagrachari and Banderban. The council consists of 22 members including the chairperson with two third of them being elected from among the tribal communities. The elected members of the Hill District Councils indirectly elect the members of the CHTRC.[54]

Power & Functions of the Regional Council:[55]

The following are the major functions of the Regional Council:

(a) The council shall supervise and co-ordinate the subjects vested under the Hill District Councils (dealt later on) including co-ordination of all development activities conducted under the three Hill District Councils, local Councils including the CHT Development Board and the Municipalities in discharging their responsibilities;

(b) The CHTRC may also co-ordinate and supervise in matters of general administration, law and order and development of the three Hill Districts, and the activities of the NGOs along with conducting and management of natural calamities and relief works

(c) The Regional Council has the power of issuing license for heavy industry.

Article 9(a), Part C of the peace accord also states that the decision of the CHTRC shall be final when the Hill Districts Councils (HDC) fails to coordinate among them.

Composition of the Hill District Councils

The HDC of each of the three districts of the CHT is consists of 31 members including the chairperson (who is to be elected from among tribal communities) with three seats reserved for women. The 'eligible voters', who reside in the CHT shall elect the members of the HDCs through direct enfranchise. Who are the eligible voters?

Article 9 of Part B of the accord states that a citizen of Bangladesh, who by virtue of permanent domicile in any of the three HDCs and who has attained the age of 18 years and is declared as mentally sound by any competent court qualifies to be an eligible voter.

Functions and Responsibilities of the Hill District Council

Land and land management, the CHT police with members consisting of the rank of sub-inspector and below, tribal law and social justice, youth welfare, environmental protection and development, local councils, improving trust and other local government institutions, issue of license to local industries and business, water resources management accepting the Kaptai lake, proper use and irrigation of other rivers and canals and beefs, preservation of statistics of birth and deaths, business transactions and jhum cultivation are the subjects included within the administrative jurisdiction of the HDCs.

Beside these, under Article 33, Part A of the accord, the HDCs have the right to provide vocational training and primary education in mother tongue.

Under Article 26(3) of Part B of the peace accord, the council can supervise and control functions of Village Headman, Chairman Amin, Surveyor, Kanungo and Assistant Commissioner (land).

Evaluation of the Post Accord CHT's Administration in Term of good governance

Good governance may be defined as process of administration, which is based on the rules of democracy, respects for human rights and emphasizes on transparency and efficiency in public administration.

According P.R.Chari, an administration is said to good governance, when it includes the following features.[56]

i. promotion of efficiency and transparency in public administration,

ii. respect for human rights and the rule of law and

iii. greater role for the civilian bodies in monitoring and managing the security sector

Public Administration at Work in the CHT

The post accord administration of the CHT is divided along ethnic and communal lines. The Muslim Bengalis feel that they have not been adequately represented in the CHTRC. Therefore, they argue that the peace accord ignored their fundamental rights. Nevertheless, they have been successful in developing and running a parallel administration vis-à-vis the CHTRC in cooperation with the civil servants (Deputy Commissioner and Upazila Nirbahi Officer) posted in the CHT. The police and the military institutions, and Mr. Wadud Bhuiyan[57] publicly back this parallel administration. The ethnic and communal polarization in the CHT administration brings these two forms of administration into often clash of interests along communal lines.

The peace-accord also divided the Jummas into two rival groups with one group (PCJSS, the signatory to the accord) supporting and campaigning for implementation of the accord and another group (UPDF) denouncing it and campaigning for 'Full Autonomy'.[58] Often antagonism and belligerency between these two groups resulted into regular armed clashes between the armed cadres of the JSS and the UPDF. The armed cadres of both groups have also been running parallel administration at certain level especially in the Jumma inhabited areas with regular extortion, abduction and killing the supporters of the opposition group.

Another distressing feature the CHT's administration is the presence of corrupt elements in the governing apparatus. Taking bribes, tax evasion, smuggling and other economic offences have been politicized along party's lines in such a way that the offenders have never been apprehended and prosecuted. The poor cultivators have to bribe the dealing officers while taking agricultural loans from Agricultural Bank of Bangladesh, and even while attempting to register their possessed lands. Infact, corruption in the CHT reached at such level that people do not hesitate to bribe more than Tk. one lakh (equivalent to almost Rupees seventy thousands) for a post of assistant teacher in a primary school.[59]

Criminalization of politics in the CHT is another dismal feature in the post accord CHT's administration. The entry and infiltration of the criminals into governing apparatus with overt or covert backing of the politicians led to criminalization of politics in the CHT. The BNP, AL, JSS and even UPDF have all taken shelter of this form of politics in their attempt to retain or expand their influence in the politics of the CHT. The nexus between the pillars of government and anti-social elements has beeen affecting largely the smooth functioning of the CHT's governance.

Human Rights Situation and Rule of Law in the CHT

Virtually there is no rule of law and respect for human rights in the CHT. The division of the post accord CHT administration along ethnic and communal lines led to the occurrence of communal violence between the Bengali settlers and the Jummas several times. For instance, violence occurred on 16 October 1998 where two innocent Jummas were killed. More than 100 had been wounded and dozen of Jumma houses and shops had been ransacked before they were set ablaze.60 On 18th May 2001 another communal riot took place in Diginala. The Bengali settlers backed by the military and paramilitary forces attacked three returnee Jumma refugee villages—namely Shanti— Laxmipur, Kalachan Mahajanpara and Hemabrata Karbaripara of Chhoto Merung Union under Diginala Thana (Police Station). Five Jumma women-Nomita Chakma (20), Panchalika Chakma (22), Surobala Chakma (55), Suchitra Chakma (30) and Savitri Chakma were wounded. The settlers also looted and burnt to ashes to 42 Jumma houses.[61] In a similar incident between 24 and 25 September 2003, the settlers with the backing of military and Para-military forces attacked and burnt to ashes more than 500 Jumma houses in Mahalchari Bazar under Khagrachari district of the CHT. The mob had beaten to death to Mr. Binod Bihari Kisha. The incident took place following the abduction of Mr. Rupam Mahajan, a local Hindu Bengali businessperson at Mahalchari bazar allegedly by the UPDP.[62]

Abduction and rape of Jumma women is another common form of human rights abuses against the women in the CHT. For instance, on 22 May 2001, in the name of flushing out 'terrorists', a group of Bangladesh army from Durgabari Camp under Guimara Brigade harassed and tortured many Jumma villagers indiscriminately and raped 3 Jumma women – Purbali Tripura (23), Karandi Tripura (20) and Sunita Tripura (16).[63]

The intra-Jumma armed conflicts deteriorated the human security environment in the Jummas inhabited areas of the CHT. It increased suspicion and distrust among the Jummas in such a way that they cannot move freely.

Role of the Civilian Institutions in Managing and Monitoring the Security Sector

The civilian bodies such as the CHTRC, and the HDCs have little role in managing and monitoring the security sector in the CHT. Although democratic institutions have been reinstated in Bangladesh following the 1992 democratic election, the military authority continues to exercise their dominance over the CHT's administration (civil and political). For instance, in the name of operation 'Uttaran' (Operator Elevation), the military authority intervened and constrained the scope of smooth functioning of the administration. The military institution also interferes in renovation and constructions of roads and controls law and order and meddles over the selection of Jumma students seeking admission for higher education in engineering and medical colleges. They are still encouraging settlement of Bengali settlers in the region through 'Shantakaran' (pacification) projects in total contravention of the CHT peace accord. In the name of maintaining law and order situation (without sanction of the civilian institutions), they continue to torture and harass the innocent Jumma people by checking the passenger buses and vehicles and interrogating the passengers.

There are several factors, which annihilated the Jummas in the post accord political and civil administration of the CHT.

I. Non-implementation of the CHT Peace-Accord:

The GoB is yet to implement the following fundamental points of the CHT peace accord:

(a) Ineffectiveness and non-functioning of the Land Commission:

Article 4 of Part D of the CHT peace-accord laid down the formation of a Land Commission headed by a retired justice for settling land disputes. The commission has been empowered to cancel ownership of those lands/ hills, which have so far been illegally settled and occupied on the basis existing rules, customs and usages in the CHT [Article 16(B)]. It also stated that the judgment and decision of the commission should be final.

The GoB, instead of making the commission functioning and effective, it promulgated another controversial "Land-Disputes Settlement Act of 2001" in 2001 in violation of Article 4 and Article 6(b), Part D of the accord. Much against the original treaty provision, the Act emphasizes that in case of controversy among the members on any land dispute, the decision shall be final. No appeal can be made against the judgment in any court of law. The Act also considered the land-disputes of only those refugees who had been repatriated under the agreement of 1997 signed at Agartala between the GoB's delegation and refugee leaders. It did not consider the land disputes of the refugees repatriated in 1992 and of those displaced internally.[64]

(b) Non-Withdrawal of Military and Para-military Camps from the CHT:

Under Article 17, Part D of the peace-agreement the GoB requires to take back all the temporary camps of military, Ansar and Village Defence Party (VDP) to permanent installations accept BDR and permanent cantonments (3 of the 3 District Hqs. and Alikadam, Ruma and Diginala) in phases following improvement of the situation. However, out of the 520 temporary camps, the GoB dismantled only 31.[65]

(c) Control over Participation of the Jumma Civil Societies in Development Activities:

The GoB in 1999-2000 formed an NGO Bureau to control and supervise the development activities of the NGOs. The Bureau made it mandatory for every NGO to obtain permission for any development activity with foreign funds. The Jumma Civil Society alleges that the government has been pursuing a discriminatory policy towards the Jummas using the

NGO Bureau as a device to control their developmental activities. They allege that the Bureau is lenient towards Bengali NGOs like the Bangladesh Rural Advancement Committee (BRAC) and Prosika and national and international Islamic NGOs such as the Bangladesh Islamic Foundation and Al Rabeta.

Extension of the Bureau's power of controlling and supervising the development activities in the CHT violates Article 9(A) of Part C of the peace-accord. Further, appointment of Mr. Wadud Bhuiyan, MP of the Khagrachari district as the Chairman of the CHTDB is a violation of Article 10 of Part C of the Peace-accord.

(d) Non-Formation of CHT Police Force:

According to Article 24(A), Part B of the peace-accord, the CHTRC has been empowered to form a Hill District Police Force with members in and below the rank of sub-inspector. However, the government is yet to implement this vital provision of the accord.

(e) Control over Civil Administration:

The civil administration in the CHT mainly constitutes with officers of 3 Deputy Commissioners (DC), the district administrators of 3 Hill Districts and 25 TNO's. Article 18 of Part D of the peace-accord laid down that permanent residents of CHT, on priority basis to the tribal, should be appointed to all posts of officers and employees at all levels of government, semi-government, council offices and autonomous bodies in the CHT. However, the government continues to appoint Bengalis in all key administrative posts such as DC, and TNO in violation to this Article of the accord. Presently, all the DCs of 3 Hill Districts and the TNOs of 25 Thanas in the CHT are Bengalis.

(f) Neglect of the Ministry of the CHT Affairs:

Article 19 of Part D, CHT peace-accord laid down the formation of Ministry for CHT affairs under an independent charge of a Jumma Minister having the status of State Minister. However, the BNP led GoB had appointed Mr. Moni Swapan Dewan as Deputy Minister in the Ministry in violation of above Article. Without holding election, the BNP led GoB unilaterally appointed the Chairmen of the three Hill District Councils in total contravention of Article 4b (3), Part B of the accord. It also undermined the multiparty democratic fabric of the CHT.

II. Constitutional Denial of Separate Identity of the Jummas

One of the fundamental demands of the Jumma people is constitutional recognition of their distinct identity. However, the peace-accord failed to address and establish this fundamental demand and concern of the Jumma people. The Bangladesh's constitution continues to recognize Islam as the only religion and Bengali as the only language in the country.

There are also many reasons behind non-implementation of peace accord. In the first place, the CHT peace accord lacks constitutional recognition. The accord was concluded without constitutional amendment. Therefore, the GoB retains the right to amend or declare it annulled with a simple parliamentary resolution. The GoB has taken full advantage to the absence of legal validation of the peace accord. For instance, the Law Ministry of Bangladesh on 12 April 1998 presented before the Parliament the Bills of Amendment of some laws of HDCs. These amendment Bills suggested for great changes on the existing laws in the HDCs. It brought inconsistency with many provisions (stated above) of the CHT peace-accord. Secondly, the CHT peace-accord was concluded without involvement, mediation, or intervention of any third party. As there is absence of third party's monitoring on the implementation process or international pressure on the GoB, instead of implementing, it is rather violating many vital provisions (stated earlier) of the CHT peace-accord. Thirdly, the major political parties of Bangladesh such as BNP, AL, JP-E, and Islamic Akkho Jot (united front) do not have consensus on the CHT peace-accord. Therefore, no political party could take bold decision in implementing the peace-accord. Fourthly, the GoB has taken full advantage of internal armed clashes between JSS and UPDF especially in matters related to implementation of the peace-accord. Finally, the root cause of the CHT political crisis lies in the implantation of thousands of settlers in the CHT from various plain districts of Bangladesh. Hence, a clearly defined treaty provision is required to determine the future status of the politically implanted settlers in the CHT. The CHT peace-accord lacks such a legal definition on the status of the settlers in the CHT in the post-accord period. Article 9 of Part B laid down that among other things, a person to be eligible as a voter in the CHT should be a permanent resident in any of the three districts.

All the thirteen ethnic minority groups of the CHT or the Jummas are permanent tribal residents by virtue of their permanent domicile in any of the three HDCs. Now who are 'non-tribal permanent residents in the CHT?

Article 3 of Part B of the peace-accord provides that any non-tribal person, who is living at a certain address by possessing land legally in the Hill District, shall be treated as 'non-tribal permanent resident'.

Most of the settlers possess registered lands. They have also been generally living at a certain address in any of the three Hill Districts. Therefore, shall they be treated as 'non-tribal permanent residents' in the CHT?

To look at the answer of this question, we need to verify whether their possessed lands have legal ownership or not. Now most of the settlers have legal ownership over their possessed lands. However, the Jummas allege they do not have any legal ownership. The settlers in most cases forcefully grabbed the Jummas' lands in total contravention of the 1900 CHT Manual. To look into this controversy and land disputes, the CHT peace-accord laid down formation of a land commission. Article 6(a) of Part D of the accord stated that the commission should settle all land disputes according to the "existing" rules, customs and usages of the CHT. The question is—what did this Article mean by the terms *'existing rules, customs and usages of the CHT'*? Did it mean the traditional rules, customs or usages established and made operational and effective in the CHT after the abolition of the CHT Manual of 1900? Hence, ambiguity remains whether the settlers are voters or not. The JSS based on its own interpretation i.e. connoting the term 'existing' as traditional, justifies disqualifying the settlers as eligible voters in the CHT. On the contrary, the settler-backed parallel administration in the CHT justifies inclusion of all the settlers in the voter list based on its own legal interpretation of the term 'existing' and Article 36 and 42(I) of the Bangladesh Constitution. The accord should have incorporated the world 'traditional/customary' in place of 'existing' to remove this legal contradiction in determining the status of the settlers.

Conclusion

Absence of good governance is the most striking feature in the politics of the CHT today. The CHT post-accord political environment possesses all the features of the pre-accord political environment. Rather the situation has become more complicated than what it was before the peace accord. It proves that the CHT peace accord has failed to achieve its preferred goals. However, for an amicable and long lasting solution, the following points may be considered:

i. Since implementation of the peace accord is pre-eminent, the GoB must implement it immediately. In addition to this, the GoB needs to accord constitutional recognition to the CHTRC and transfer more powers without endangering and questioning the territorial integrity of the country,

ii. That the GoB should also give constitutional recognition to all the thirteen ethnic national minorities as separate identities by a Constitutional amendment in Article 3 of Part I of its Bangladesh's Constitution,

iii. That to determine the legal residential status of the politically implanted settlers in the CHT, both parties of the conflict requires a consensus and understands each other's position. For the purpose, the following options may be tried: a) Fixing a year based on consensus some settlers can be resettled back with onerous compensation and rehabilitation outside the CHT to reduce the percentage of Muslim population in the CHT. b) By settling down all the existing land disputes between the settlers and Jummas on a mutually compromised formula, the settlers may be given legal residential right in the CHT with enactment of a law restricting for further settlement. c) Comprising areas of the existing three districts in the CHT, another HDC may be created. Some settler's families from these existing three Hill districts can be resettled and rehabilitated in the newly created district and made more representation in proposed HDC for their equal representation. d) Choice and appointment of minister to the Ministry of CHT Affairs should not be a prerogative of the Prime Minister and the Ministry should not be used as an institutional tool to control and disrupt the functioning of the CHT civil administration. e) Affected parties like India and Myanmar and international institutions like the United Nations may be involved in the peace-process and monitor the development of the situation based on an agreement.

NOTES AND REFERENCES

1. Mr. Mukut Khanti Khisa was a career diplomat and represented India as ambassador in many countries before he retired from service in 1997. He was born in Khagrachari district of the CHT in 1935 in a traditional Chakma family, received his education from Presidency College of Kolkatta before he joined Indian Foreign Service. Mr. Chakma was an ardent supporter of the CHT's merger with the Union of India in 1947.
2. Based on my interviews and interactions with and e-mails received from hundred selected Jummas from Arunachal Pradesh, Mizoram, Tripura, West Bengal (Kolkata) India, and French and the CHT of Bangladesh dividing them into four different groups Viz. student, politician, scholar and service holders. Accept a few of all the respondents (mostly from the CHT who do not have clear ideas about India's political-administrative system), every one told the scholar that their interests would have been better served and promoted had the CHT been integrated with the Union of India in 1947.
3. This is based on the figures shown by the Chittagong Hill Tracts Peoples Association (CHTPA) in a memorandum to the United Nations organization, 24 January 1948. For further reference, see Subir Bhaumik, " Stategic Pawn: Indian Policy in the CHT, in Subir Bhaumik et. Al., *Living on the Edge: Essays on the Chittagong Hill Tracts,* Kathmandu: South Asia Forum for Human Rights, 1997, p. 139.
4. As stated in Amena Mohsin, *The Politics of Nationalism: The Case of the Chittagong Hill Tracts, Bangladesh,* Dhaka: The University Press Limited, 1997, p.36.
5. *Ibid.*, pp. 36-37. Also see The CHT Commission, *Life is not ours: Land and Rights in the CHT, Bangladesh,* Netherlands, 1995, p. 12.
6. The Government of Mizoram took the shelter of India's Citizenship Laws for disenfranchising the Chakmas branding them as foreigners. However, the Government failed to identify foreigners from among the Chakmas. Nevertheless, due to historical animosity between the Lushai (Mizo) and the Chakma communities, the Government deleted the names of many eligible Chakma voters from the voter list. For instance, in the revised voter list of 1998, the Government of Mizoram deleted the name of Mr. Nirupam Chakma, who

has been elected twice to the Legislative Assembly of Mizoram.

7. The Indigenous Peoples Front of Tripura (IPFT) came to power at Tripura Tribal Area District Council (TTADC) in 1998 fully with the covert backing of the National Liberation Front of Tripura (NLFT). It merged with Indigenous Peoples Front of Tripura (INPT) and fought the Tripura Legislative Assembly's election in 2002 with the backing of the NLFT in alliance with the Congress party. The party however could not show better result as expected.
8. It is of course undeniable that majority of the Chakmas of Tripura have been migrated to Tripura during and after partition of the Indian sub-continent. However, Tripura had substantial number of Chakma population ever before the partition. For details, see the population census reports in Tripura available in Tribal Research Institute of Tripura, Agartala.
9. As cited in Mohsin, *op. cit.*, p. 37.
10. Under Rule 51 of the CHT Manual, the administration of the CHT has the right to expel the non-hill people from the CHT.
11. Rule 54 of the Manual restricted non-hill people to enter into the CHT without obtaining prior permission from the Deputy Commissioner of the Chittagong Division.
12. Rule 34 of the Manual imposed restrictions on the possession of lands by outsiders in the CHT.
13. It generated employment opportunities for the Bengali (the hill people did not have any participation in the project) and served the commercial interests of the Bengali businesspersons in various ways. The hill people allege that although electricity is generated from the Kaptai hydroelectric project, most parts of the CHT remain dark without electricity. Besides, economic opportunities generated by the project encouraged Bengali immigration within the CHT from the plain districts of Bangladesh. This has been said to the scholar by Mr. Mukur Kanti Kisha, a retired Indian diplomat, Mr. Babatosh Dewan, a top leader of undivided PCJSS, Ven. Bimal Bhikkhu, a social worker and many others including experts on the CHT political crisis during formal and informal interactions with them. For further reference, see, Mohsin, *op.cit.*, pp. 102-105, Mohammad Humayun Kabir, "The Problem of Tribal Separatism and Constitutional Reforms in Bangladesh", in Iftekharuzzama (ed.), *Ethnicity and Constitutional Reform in South Asia*, New Delhi: Manohar, 1998, p. 16.

14. *Ibid.*, pp. 102-04.
15. Stated in *Population Transfer and Implantation of Bengali Settlers: The Threat of Survival of the Jumma People*, New Delhi: Jumma People Network (JNP) of South Asia Coordination Section, 6 April 1998, pp. 16-18.
16. Apart from the Jummas of the CHT, there are also many indigenous communities living in the plain districts of Bangladesh. For instance, Garo and Kashi communities live in the Shylet division. Shantal and Oraon live with huge numbers in the Rajshahi division of Bangladesh. These communities also face similar problems like the Jummas in the CHT.
17. Sheikh Mujibur Rahman reiterated this in the course of parliamentary debate, as quoted in Mohsin, *op. cit.*, p. 59.
18. *Ibid.*, p. 62.
19. *Ibid.*, p. 61.
20. Since the implantation of settlers in the CHT, several communal riots took place. In all these riots, most of the victims were Jummas because the civil-military administration fully backed the settlers in carrying out such savageries against the Jummas. For details about the number of persons killed and wounded in those riots, see Mohsin, *op.cit.*, pp. 182-84.
21. *Ibid.*, p. 166. Also see, Aftab Ahmed, "Ethnicity and Insurgency in the Chittagong Hill Tracts Region: A Study of the Crisis of Political Integration in Bangladesh"; *Journal of Commonwealth and Comparative Politics*, Vol. XXXI, No. 3, 1993, p. 46.
22. *Ibid.*, p. 172.
23. *Ibid.*
24. The CHT Commission, *op. cit.*, p. 4.
25. See Iftekharuzzam (ed.), *op. cit.*, pp. 17-18.
26. See A.S. Narang, *Indian Government and Politics*, New Delhi: Gitanjali Publishing House, 1997, pp. 58-5
27. Aditya Kumar Dewan, *Class and Ethnicity in the Hills of Bangladesh*, an unpublished Ph.D. dissertation paper, Mc-Gill University, 1990, pp. 456-58.
28. During my visits to the CHT in 1995 and 1998, I have observed that most of the settlers' concentrations are located nearby the camps of the security forces. Thus for attacking the security forces, the SB had to launch military assault first at the settlers' concentrations. It also helped the GoB to launch offensive national and international electronic media

campaign against the SB for killing the innocent settlers.

29. For details about the hill people and Bengali population statistics in the CHT see, B.H. Suhrawardy, Outline of the CHT Economy: An Analysis, in Arunendu Tripura et. al.; *Vision*, Rangamati, 15 June 1995, p. 38. In fact, the policy of population transfer into the CHT from the plain districts is still effective even in the post accord phage. Jumma leaders, Mr. Santu Larma, President of the PCJSS and Chairman of the CHTRC and Mr. Prosit Bikash Kisha, President of the UPDF allege that Mr. Wadud Bhuiyan, MP of the Kgahrachari district, is encouraging settlement of thousands more Bengalis from the CHT from the plain districts in order to increase the ratio of Bengali voters against the number of voters of the hill peoples to help him retaining the seat in every Parliamentary Election.
30. See Rajkumari Chandra Kalindi Roy, *Land Rights of the Indigenous Peoples of the Chittagong Hill Tracts, Bangladesh*, Copenhagen: IWGIA Document No. 99, 2000, p. 114.
31. As per the traditional law of the hill people, they do not generally have to register their lands against their names. That is, without any official record, they enjoy the right of ownership and occupation of their lands already under their respective occupation. So, most of the hill people do not have official documents to claim the legal ownership of their possessed lands. This system is also still effective in certain areas of some Northeastern Indian states like Arunachal Pradesh, Tripura (in the TTADEC Area).
32. The CHT is the only region of Bangladesh where the Government of independent Bangladesh first faced the problem of insurgency and the challenge of its political integration. Thousands of military and paramilitary forces had been deployed there to deal with the situation. Although, since the time of Sheikh Mujibur Rahman, the Government of Bangladesh took it as a challenge to its political integration, General Hossain Muhammad Ershad was the first ruler, who officially recognized it as national problem of Bangladesh. All his later successors followed him in treating the CHT political crisis as a national problem of Bangladesh.
33. Based on my observation and interactions with some Jumma students during a visit to Bangladesh in 1998. I noticed such banners and posters during my visit to Bangladesh in 1998. I also had some interactions with some Jumma students about the same.

34. For instance, the leaders of the UPDF argue that the PCJSS could have entered into such an agreement with the BNP too. They even argue that BNP wanted to provide more powers to the Jummas. However, the PCJSS remained adamant in its position on the Five Point Demands. The allegation may be true. In the politics of Bangladesh then, the AL regained its popularity. The General Election of Bangladesh was about to be held. Historically AL is friendly to India. India's influence in the politics of CHT remained high at that time. Moreover, AL's popularity among the Jummas then was also very high. Therefore, considering circumstances, the PCJSS, from strategic point of view perhaps could not enter into an agreement with the BNP led GoB although it showed flexible attitude for an onerous solution of the CHT political crisis. The leaders of UPDF argue that BNP opposes the peace accord mainly for this reason. The allegation of 'total sell out of the country's territory' is nothing other than a political strategy in the game of contemporary power politics of Bangladesh.
35. The Bengali settler's leaders point out that inadequate representation of the Bengalis in the HDCs and the CHTRC, declaration of the CHT as tribal area, reservation of the higher posts of these councils for the tribal are the important provisions that have infringed their democratic rights in the CHT.
36. Since BNP and Islamic Akkyo Jote jointly led agitation against the Peace accord, the BNP led GoB lacked more sincerity and commitment in implementing the peace accord. The GoB now says that although it will not scrap the accord, it will amend many provisions, which are, according to it, inconsistent with the Bangladesh's constitution.
37. Bhaumik, *op. cit.* pp. 279-81.
38. For details about patricidal killings among the Jummas in the post accord situation in the CHT, see ***www.amidatrust.com/CHT_update_2.htm***; Elusive Peace in the Chittagong Hill Tracts in ***www.aitpn.org/research.html;*** Sona Ram Chakma, Chittagong Hill Tracts: Peace is still elusive in *www.updfcht.org*.
39. For instance, Mohammad Humayun Kabir, "The Problem of Tribal Separatism and Constitutional Reforms in Bangladesh", in Iftekharuzzam, (ed.), *Ethnicity and Constitutional Reforms in South Asia*, New Delhi: Manohar, 19998, pp. 16-18. Also see, Isanul Haq, "Ethnicity and Political Separatism in the Chittagong Hill Tracts of Bangladesh", Dhaka: University Press Limited, 1998, pp. 30-31.

40. See Sumantra Bose, *States, Nations, Sovereignty: Srilanka, India and the Tamil Eelam Movement*, New Delhi: Sage Publications, 1994, pp. 30-31.
41. Ibid, p. 31.
42. Paul R. Brass, *Ethnicity and Nationalism: Theory and Comparison*, New Delhi: Sage Publications, 1991, p. 20.
43. Mohsin, *op.cit.*, pp. 57-58.
44. Bhaumik, *op. cit.*, p. 258.
45. For details, see the Charter of the Modified Five Point Demand of the PCJSS, a Publication of the *Department of Information and Publicity of the PCJSS*, 15 August 1996.
46. See the Primary Declaration of the UPDF, 26 December 1998.
47. As stated in Suhas Chakma, *Time Out of Hand*, New Delhi: Asian Indigenous and Tribal Peoples Network, 2003, p. 14.
48. *Ibid.*
49. Erica-Irene A. Daes is the Chairperson of the Working Group on Indigenous Population.
50. *Ibid.*, p. 15.
51. For details see Maivan Clech Lam, "At the Edge of State: Indigenous Peoples and Self Determination", *Transnational*, Ardsley NY, 2000, pp. 200-43. See Benedict Kingsbury, "Indigenous Peoples in International Law: A Constructive Approach to the Asian Controversy", in *American Journal of International Law*, Vol. 92, Issue 3, July 1998, pp. 438-39.
52. *Ibid.*
53. Although the GoB does not recognize the existence of indigenous peoples in Bangladesh, the Jummas claim themselves as indigenous people within the legal framework of international definitions of indigenous peoples. For international definitions on indigenous peoples, see Roy, *op. cit.*, pp. 419-21.
54. For details see the draft of the Peace Accord of 1997 between the PCJSS and the Government of Bangladesh in Saradindu Mukerji, "*Subjects, Citizens and Refugees: Tragedy in the Chittagong Hill Tracts (1947-1998)*, New Delhi: Indian Centre for the Study of Forced Migration, 2000, p. 223.
55. *Ibid.*, p. 234.
56. P.R. Chari, "Security and Governance in South Asia: Their Linkages", in P.R. Chari (ed.) *Security and Governance in South Asia*, New Delhi: Manohar, 2001, p. 14.
57. Mr. Wadud Bhuiayn is a Bengali settler. He has been elected as MP to the Bangladesh National Assembly in 2002 General Election as a BNP candidate from the Khagrachari constituency.

58. See the Primary Declaration of the UPDF, *op. cit*.
59. This is based on my interview on corruption in the CHT with Basu Dev Chakma, Nion Dewan, Jyostna Khati Dewan and Sashwata Priyo Chakma. They are all students from the CHT who were studying in Delhi during 2002-2003.
60. Peace Campaign Group, "A Report on the Demonstration against the Government of Bangladesh at Paris Consortium 2002," New Delhi: Peace Campaign Group, 10 April 2002, p. 14.
61. *Ibid*.
62. *Mayhem at Mahalchari*, a report on the Mahalchari incident of 2003, prepared by the UPDF.
63. Peace Campaign Group, *op. cit*., p. 15. Also, see *The Swadikar*, a periodical news bulletin of the UPDF, July 2001.
64. Peace campaign Group, *op. cit*., pp. 7-8.
65. *Ibid*., p. 10.

3

The Chittagong Hill Tracts Political Crisis and India's National Security: Internal and External Dimension

This chapter would attempt to look at how the CHT political crisis impinges on India's national security with special reference to the security environment of Tripura. The chapter is divided into three sections while going into details about this part of the dissertation. The first section deals with how the CHT has been a sanctuary to various Northeast insurgent groups from time to time. Here it argues that the Northeast insurgent groups generally use the CHT not only as base, but also in planning and execution of subversive operations against Indian security establishments in the Northeast. This section further argues that it is through the CHT, the insurgent groups meet the purpose of arms smuggling and establishing external nexus with various foreign intelligent agencies. While analyzing the impact of these anti Indian activities on India's national security, it argues that Northeast insurgency in league with external powers seriously threatened India's political and geographical integration with the Northeast region in the 1970s. Ethnic insurgency now does not threaten India's territorial integrity. However, it stands as serious impediment in national political integration and establishing good governance in the Northeast. The second section attempts to look at the trend of Islamization and the rise of Islamic fanaticism in Bangladesh in general and the CHT in particular. It opines that the intensity of Islamization and the rise of Islamic fanaticism are very high in Bangladesh in general and the CHT in particular. Such a development in Bangladesh is a threat to India's national, regional as well as international interests. The last section deals with the problem of refugees generated into India from the CHT and its repercussions on national and regional politics and the economy of India as well.

I

THE CHITTAGONG HILL TRACTS POLITICAL CRISIS AND THE NORTHEAST INSURGENCY: THEIR LINKAGES

Before establishing the linkages between the CHT political crisis and Northeast insurgency, we would attempt to look at how the Northeast insurgents groups used the CHT as their base in guerilla training, planning and execution of anti Indian activities in different parts of India.

NSCN-(IM), NSCN-(K), PLA, UNLF, ULFA, NDFB, ATTF and NLFT are the names of several insurgent groups, which are still active in different parts of Northeast. With the exception of NSCN (K), UNLF and NDFB, all the other insurgent groups have used and continue to use the CHT as their main base in launching anti Indian operations in the region. The Naga National Council (NNC) formed by Phizo and Mizo National Front (MNF) also used the CHT as primary base in their guerilla warfare against Indian security establishments. As noted above, it is through the CHT, these insurgent groups established external political nexus with then India's unfriendly nations like the USA, China, Pakistan, and international human rights organizations like Amnesty International, Survival International etc. For instance, Mr. Sainghaka, a prominent leader in the history of Mizo insurgency, in an interview revealed about the political nexus between the Mizo insurgency and the Pakistani external intelligence agency—Inter-Service Intelligence (ISI) in the following language:[1]

> Senior Pakistani intelligence officers told us that we would have no problem so long as we fought India. One of the officers was a brigadier, who promised us bases inside the CHT, and said that the Chinese were agreeable to assist us through Pakistan. We were given a number of contact codes and asked to set up groups of volunteers who could be organized for guerilla warfare on the Naga pattern. The plan was delayed because of Laldenga's arrest but was revived immediately after his release. It was a case of now and never.

Similarly, Mr. Lalhningthanga, MNF's Foreign Minister, in another interview, disclosed about the politico-military nexus between the Chinese government and MNF. He described it in the following statement:[2]

> The Chinese promised to send us large quantities of weapons through Pakistan. They also agreed to train some MNF guerillas to fight a "people war" on the Chinese model. We agreed to send a batch of guerillas to China. However, when we asked them to recognize the MNF Government, they refused.

The above two statements proved that Pakistan and China were overtly and covertly involved in the Northeast insurgency. China might not have accorded de-jure sovereign political status to the MNF government. However, like Pakistan, it also instigated and sophisticated the Northeast insurgency by providing psychological, political and arms support in the 2nd half of 1970s and beginning of 1980s.

During this period, many Western diplomats as well as international human rights organizations also expressed their sympathy for the Naga and Mizo causes by calling them as "persecuted Christians".[3] Following the footsteps of the Naga and Mizo insurgency, many disenchanted groups also started insurgency movement in Tripura, Manipur and Assam. The geographical isolation of Northeast from the main land, politico-military nexus between the Northeast insurgency and the Sino-Pakistani axis and Western sympathy garnered by the movement for its religious proximity with the Western world alarmed and worried the India's policy makers about political and geographical integration of North east with mainland

India. India's military power might take up and neutralize the security threat posed by such insurgency. Nevertheless, India had to consider other security-related developments in the politics of South Asia. Pakistan entered into various US's led military alliances like SEATO, CENTO. The US also started arming Pakistan. The Sino-Pakistani political and strategic proximity, particularly after the 1962 Sino-Indian border war developed widely. Besides, China's heavy militarization in Tibet continued even after the1962 border skirmishes. It established military facilities in the Chumbi Valley, a forward area, very close to the Zalpaiguri district of West Bengal. It is the only geographical landmass that connects the Northeast with the mainland India. Geographically then, the entire Northeast appeared isolated from the mainland as the Sino-Pakistani military nexus and the Northeast insurgent groups had strategically almost encircled Northeast India. A joint Sino-Pakistani preemptive military strike could bring heavy security repercussions on India at that juncture of South Asia's security environment.

Now the questions are- what was the linkage between the then Northeast insurgency and the political movement of the hill people of the CHT? Why did Pakistan, China and the USA meddled in India's Northeast's affairs by supporting the Northeast insurgency?

Political movement of the hill people of the CHT began within the politics of Pakistan itself. The movement just reached at a new momentum in Bangladesh's period. As stated in the second chapter, the Pakistan did not see positively the pro-Indian agitation of the hill people during partition. That is why it amended the CHT manual of 1900, made the CHT an ordinary district of Bengal and constructed a big hydroelectric dam on the Karnafulli River for annihilating them politically and destroying the backbone of their economy beyond reparation. Pakistan however did not stop there. It backed the Mizo and the Naga insurgency and allowed them to use its soils, particularly the CHT. Why did the Pakistani regime back cross border insurgency against India? Why did it choose the CHT as the epicenter of backing cross border insurgency?

Pakistan's relations with India did not start in a friendly diplomatic gesture. Hostility based on misperception and misunderstanding marked India and Pakistan relations since their creation in 1847. Pakistan did not welcome the British administration's decision conferring Kashmir with the power of deciding its political future. It wanted Kashmir's forceful merger if Kashmir did not voluntarily join with Pakistan. However, Pakistan failed to integrate Kashmir even after the first Indo-Pakistani war on Kashmir in 1947-48. Instead, India by a constitutional amendment integrated Kashmir into the Union of India. This humiliation of the Pakistani regime in India's hand hardened its anti Indian position and encouraged to instigate violent anti Indian activities in many parts of India, more particularly in Jammu and Kashmir in and the Northeast India. The contemporary Pakistani regime realized that the Nagas and the Mizos already launched political movement against India's rule. Therefore, it had chosen to encourage and back cross border insurgency against India in the Northeast.

As far as the second question is concerned, Pakistan government knew the historical animosity between the Mizos and the Chakmas, the dominant ethnic group in the CHT. Pakistan wanted to utilize the hostility between these two communities in its covert war against India. This silent war against India had two objectives. It wanted to use cross border insurgency in the Northeast as diplomatic tool to exert political pressure on India so that it brought a change in its policy in the Kashmir. Secondly, by supporting the Mizo insurgency, it wanted to checkmate and create a political deterrence against the pro-Indian feeling present among the hill people, particularly the Chakmas in the CHT.

As noted above, the major insurgent groups of Northeast still maintain their base camps in the CHT. The CHT is now a part of Bangladesh. Bangladesh became independent only with India's help. However, despite India's wider contribution in the liberation war, why did Bangladesh like Pakistan allow the Northeast insurgent groups to use its soil against India's interests? Before we go into detailed analysis into this question, let us look at the locations of the base camps maintained by the Northeast insurgent groups in the Bangladesh in general and the CHT in particular.

The following are the major camps of the major insurgent groups of Tripura located in the CHT and other parts of Bangladesh:

1. All Tripura Tiger Force (ATTF):[4]

Sl. No.	*Name of the Camp*	*Location*
i	Khagrachari	PS. Diginala, Dist. Khagrachari, CHT

ii	Khagrapur Family HQ.	-do-
iii.	Matiranga	PS. Matiranga, Dist. Khagrachari, CHT
iv.	Taraban	PS. Panchari, Dist. Khagrachari, CHT
v.	Satchari HQ.	PS. Chanarughat, Dist. Hobiganj, Sylhet
vi.	Daluchara	-do-
vii.	Srimangal	-do-
viii.	Khasiapunji	Ps. Kamlganj, Dist. Maulavibazer, Sylhet
ix.	Machaichara	-do-

2. National Liberation Front of Tripura (Biswamohan's Faction) (NLFT-BM):[5]

Sl. No.	*Name of the Camp*	*Location*
i.	Khagrapur Camp	PS. Khagrachari Sadar, CHT
ii.	9-Mile	PS. Matiranga, Dist. Khagrachari, CHT
iii.	Sajek Family HQ.	PS. Sajek, Dist. Rangamati, CHT.
iv.	Taglakantai(Ranger Regiment.)	-do-
v.	Sajek Rest Camp	-do-
vi.	Smai(KongKong) Training Center	-do-
vii.	Ujanchari	-do-
viii.	Gil Gal	PS. Thanchi ,Dist. Banderban, CHT

ix.	Srimangal	PS. Srimangal, Dist. Maulivibazer, Sylhet
x.	Niralapunji (Khasiapunji)	PS. Kamalganj, Dist. Maulivibazer, Shylet
xi.	Thunder Regiment Camp	-do-
xii.	Ali Sahar	Chittagong Mani Town

3. National Liberation Front of Twipara ([Nayanbasi Group) (NLFT-NB):[6]

Sl. No.	*Name of the Camp*	*Location*
i.	Chunarughat (Banumara)	PS. Chunarughat, Dist. Habiganj, Sylhet
ii.	Kalanjipunji (Khasiapunji)	P.S. Kamalganj, Dist. Maulivibazer, Sylhet
iii.	Mangalji Training Camp.	-do-
iv.	Kudalia (Gajipur)	PS. Burichong, Dist. Commilla.

NSCN-IM mainly uses Maini Reserved forest (bordering with Awizal district of Mizoram and North Tripura district of Tripura). ULFA is also believed to have been running several base camps in different parts of the CHT, more particularly in the Khagrachari district.[7]

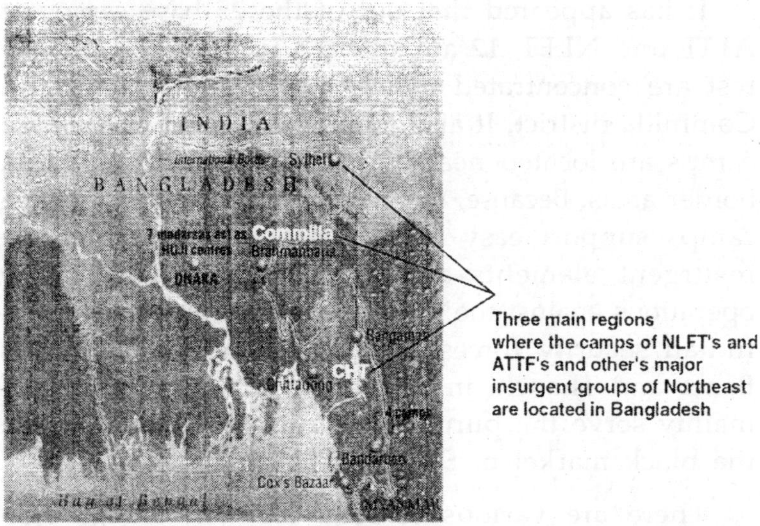

The above map indicates the locations in Bangladesh where the bases of NLFT, ATTF, NSCN-IM and ULFA are primarily concentrated. The locations in the map are pointed based on the following sources. The map is taken from *India Today,* December 9, 2002, p. 53.

Source: See, Secret, *"Extremist Camps in Bangladesh"*, a report prepared by the Research and Analysis Wing (RAW) about the locations of the Northeast insurgent groups in Bangladesh. Also see, Subir Bhaumik, *The Troubled Periphery : Crisis of India's Northeast*, a forthcoming book to be published by Penguin. Also see, Jayanta Debnath, *Santrasklanta Tripura,* Danik Sambad Publishers, Agartala, 2001, p. 304, Editorial Note of the *Statesman*, 30 November 2002, *The Hindustan Times,* New Delhi, 1 December 2002, p.1, *The Telegraph,* 12 May, 2003.

It has appeared that out of the 25 base camps of ATTF and NLFT, 12 are situated in the CHT and the rest are concentrated mostly in Shylet Division and Commilla district. It also reflects that most of the base camps are located near by the India and Bangladesh border areas. Because, the geo-strategic location of these camps support easy cross border movement of the insurgent elements and carrying their subversive operations against the targeted groups, individuals and Indian security forces. The base camps nearby Cox Bazer and Thanchi in Banderban district of the CHT mainly serve the purpose of arms procurement from the black market of South-East Asia.[8]

There are various reasons for why Bangladesh backed the Northeast insurgency. Following assassination of Sheikh Mujibur Rahman, the icon of Bangladesh liberation war, India's relations with Bangladesh had been severely deteriorated. The new regime in Bangladesh began ignoring India's interests in Bangladesh. By scrapping down India and Bangladesh friendship treaty signed during Mujib's era, Bangladesh developed friendly ties with India's strained neighbors, Pakistan and China. The influence of these nations in the politics of Bangladesh created a great challenge to India's position in South Asian affairs in general and Bangladesh in particular. Since Pakistan and China earlier backed the Northeast insurgency, they wanted to renew their contact with India's rebel groups through Bangladesh. Therefore, utilizing the hostile India and Bangladesh relations, these two India's strained neighbors instigated the Bangladeshi security establishment to back cross border insurgency in the Northeast. (It is to be mentioned here that Bangladesh during Mujib's era dismantled the terrorist infrastructure maintained by the Northeast insurgency). Secondly, India reacted vociferously against Mujib's assassination and steadfastly opposed new developments of Bangladesh in the post Mujib's era. The military came to the forefront in the politics of Bangladesh marginalizing the role of the civilian institutions. Therefore, from institutional point of view also, India did not welcome the new regime in Bangladesh. India's unfriendly gesture towards the new regime in Bangladesh further hardened its anti India's position in national and international politics. The most important factor was perhaps the new developments in the politics of the CHT. The PCJSS having being failed to achieve its political goals in constitutional ways formed Shanti Bahini (SB) to launch military operations against the security fabric of Bangladesh in the CHT. As stated in the second chapter that the GoB developed suspicion towards India for its new role in the CHT affairs. It perceived that India began helping the insurgency in the CHT by proving military and political support to the PCJSS and its military wing, the SB. Therefore, the GoB was also encouraged and determined to back India's Northeast rebel groups to meet three purposes. The first one was to gather intelligent information about the activities of SB. Secondly; it was aimed at neutralizing the military threat posed by the SB. For the purpose, it encouraged and instigated the Northeast insurgent elements, particularly the Mizos for containing the SB. Finally, it wanted to create a counter balance against India in diplomatic affairs related to the problem of cross border insurgency.

In 1997, India and Bangladesh reached at an understanding on cross border insurgency. They pledged not to shelter the each other's insurgent elements and galvanize cooperation to contain and fight jointly against this menace.[9] However, the GoB has failed largely to fulfill its obligation, as the anti Indian elements continued to use its soils in carrying anti national activities. During interrogations, many of the arrested and surrendered insurgent outfits have disclosed that they mainly receive the help of ISI and DGFI in arms procurement and planning and execution of their operations.[10] It is based on information gathered and interrogations of arrested and surrendered insurgents. On 29 January 2003, the Government of India asked its counterpart to handover its 88 wanted elements, who illegally live in Bangladesh. However, instead of co-operating with India, the GoB rather denied the presence of any Indian rebel group in its soils. It also showed its reluctance and hesitation to handover Anup Chetia, Secretary of ULFA, arrested during Sheikh Hashina led Awami League Government. Therefore, questions arise--why did the GoB deny the presence of the Indian rebel groups in its soils? Why did it fail to fulfill its commitments promised during an understanding on cross border insurgency in 1997?

The answer very is simple for the first question. Bangladesh firmly believes that the PCJSS has received political and moral support from India. India helped this organization to use the peripheral areas of Tripura and Mizoram in its guerilla operations against Bangladesh's security establishment in the CHT. However, the Government of India went on denying this accusation from time to time. The GoB also followed India in the strategy of 'denial' in covert war against each other.[11]

The GoB failed to fulfill its promise on India-Bangladesh cooperation against ethnic insurgency mainly for the following factors: In the *first place,* the political movement in the CHT is still alive. Although there are intra-Jumma armed clashes in the post accord politics of the CHT, they are not different in terms of political objectives. The GoB is still skeptical about India's role in the CHT. Bangladesh still alleges that some prominent leaders of the PCJSS did not return even after the peace accord.[12] *Secondly,* of course, the AL was in favour taking stern action against the Northeast insurgent outfits. As a measure, the AL led GoB arrested Anup Chetia and Sanjib Debverma, senior leader of ULFA and ATTF respectively. Howver, it could not continue its mission due to opposition and non-cooperation of both the BNP's and the JI'. These two political parties, especially the later one do not even hesitate to brand publicly the India's rebel groups as 'freedom fighters'. Moreover, the AL had to take into consideration its prospects in the 2001 General Election. Besides, the BNP and JI always opposed the initiative of the AL of re-establishing the traditional Indo-Bangladeshi relations founded in the early year of independence. Therefore, circumstances also deterred the AL not to show so much pro -Indian leaning and favoritism before the conclusion of the General Election of 2001. *Third* and perhaps, the most important factor is the closer proximity between the top cadres of Bangladesh's army and the Pakistani army and deep influence of the armed forces of Bangladesh with pan Islamic culture. Therefore, traditionally they are predominantly anti Indian but pro Pakistani in orientation. It is beyond doubt that the inter personnel relationship between some senior cadres of the

Bangladesh's armed forces (they had mostly earlier been part of Pakistan's army) and the Pakistan's army is very cordial.[13] Besides, although representative democracy was reinstated in Bangladesh following democratic election in 1992, the army continues to be a factor in Bangladesh's politics.. It still perceives as the only force, which can hold Bangladesh together. The Army continues to meddle in the civilian administration in the CHT where most of the base camps of the Northeast insurgents groups are located. The pro Pakistani leaning and influence of pan Islamism in the Army of Bangladesh provides an opportunity for the Northeast insurgent groups to maintain their base camps in the CHT in large number.

What is the impact of insurgency in the Northeast? Its impact is manifold. Insurgency seriously constrained and disturbed the functioning of good governance in the Northeast. It deteriorated the security environment of the region with general break down in the law and order situation. It criminalized and communalized the politics and created ethnic tensions between different communities (Nagas vs Kukis, Kukis vs Paitees in Manipur, Nagas vs Karbis in Assam, tribal vs non-tribal in Tripura etc.) It had badly affected the prospect of trade and commerce in the region. Extortion, kidnapping of targeted individuals and frequent attacks on the security forces are now most stumbling barriers for attracting and encouraging commercial investment from the national and international companies. In nutshell, it paralyzed largely the whole region in term of political and economic development.

A look at the Tripura's situation alone will provide

a discernible picture of the scenario. Insurgency problem in Tripura led to militarization of the Assam-Agartala National Highway, the lifeline the state's transport system. Hundreds of vehicles now move together with full security cover, generally trice in a day making the life in the state very dull and disgusting. Besides disrupting the state's transport system, it has also badly affected implementation educational programs, particularly in the tribal inhabited areas, where the insurgents groups successfully run a parallel de facto administration. Teachers, especially non-tribal teachers (who are considered skilled and experienced than the tribal) are always reluctant to get posting in the remote tribal areas due to security reasons. Therefore, most of the schools, which fall under the administration of the Tripura Tribal Area Autonomous District Council (TTADC) are running with insufficient number of school teachers. For instance, there are only six teachers in the Elmara High School of Sabroom Sub-division of South Tripura district. While three of them are graduate teachers, the other three are non- graduates. [14] This same picture is discernible in most of the schools located in the TTADC areas. This is one of the major factors for the presence of high drop out rate among tribal students in Tripura.[15]

The security scenario of Tripura is further explained with the help of the following tables:

The table shows us that insurgency related incidents went on increasing. In the field of the politics of violence, a total of sixty seven times exchange of gunfire between the security forces and the insurgent groups took place from 1997 to 2000. Altogether 133

Table 1

Insurgency related incidents in Tripura from April 1993 to August 2000

Year	*No. of abducted persons*	*Returned after paying ransoms*	*Persons killed in captivity*	*Disappearance cases*	*Security forces killed*
1993	96	82	9	5	12
1994	216	188	22	6	14
1995	367	227	21	19	26
1996	294	262	16	16	28
1997	158	128	16	14	49
1998	401	328	12	61	23
1999	480	325	28	131	46
2000	478	400	7	67	13

Source: Jayanta Debnath, *Santrasklanta Tripura*, Dainik Sambad Publishers: Agartala, 2001, p. 242.

security personals and 96 guerillas were killed during such exchanges of gunfire. Between 1993 and 2000, altogether 2460 persons have been abducted. While1940 of them have been returned after paying ransom, the rest have been killed in captivity. Altogether 289 persons have also been disappeared during the period.

The following table shows the figures of tribal and non-tribal persons killed and abducted by the insurgent groups between 10 April 1993 and 31 December 2000:

Table 2

Year		*Killed*			*Abducted*	
	Non Tribal	*Tribal*	*Total*	*Non Tribal*	*Tribal*	*Total*
1993	42	43	85	58	48	96
1994	37	62	99	140	76	216
1995	78	44	122	292	75	367
1996	95	21	116	27	123	294
1997	139	62	206	129	29	158
1998	132	71	211	346	55	401
1999	143	66	227	435	45	480
2000	150	57	207	802	72	478

Source: Debnath, *op. cit.*, p. 246.

The above table reflects that although insurgency movement in the state is directed mainly against the non-tribal, the numbers of tribal persons abducted and killed by the insurgents are no so less than the non-tribal victims. Rather, the tribal communities have been more affected if it is statistically analyzed in term of the ratio of tribal and non-tribal population in the state.[16]

Of course, ethnic insurgency in the Northeast now is not a big military threat to India's territorial integration. Because unlike the 1970's, powerful states like China, the UK and the USA do not have much involvement and therefore have little interests in the Northeast affairs. The leaders of the rebel groups are mostly confined with some parochial demands. For instance, the NSCN (I-M), which is considered as the mother of Northeast insurgency, instead of independence now demands for creation of greater 'Nagalim' by integrating the Naga inhabited areas of Assam, Arunachal Pradesh and Manipur with present Nagaland. Another important feature of insurgency in the Northeast is that the insurgent groups do not have solidarity among themselves. Instead, many of them are now fighting against one another. For instance, there is conflict between NSCN-(I-M) and NSCN-(K) in Nagaland, between PLA and UNLF in Manipur, between NLFT and ATTF in Tripura and between NDFB and BTLF in Assam. Such internal divisions in the rebel groups greatly helped the government of India to face and contain the problem with its military might very easily. Moreover, over the years, insurgency in the region lost public support. People at large have condemned and rejected their violent activities. Even the Tripuris in Tripura now vehemently oppose insurgency because, instead of any positive feedbacks, it rather largely affected the tribal communities in the state in their over all development. The Jamatia Huda, a tribal based religious organization particularly representing the Jamatia ethnic group, has already declared a holy war against tribal insurgency in Tripura.

However, despite a remarkable decline in the Northeast insurgency, it continues to disrupt normal life in the region. It continues to be formidable threat to human security in the region.

II

ISLAMIZATION AND THE RISE OF ISLAMIC FANATICISM IN THE CHT

Fundamentalism and religious intolerance always threaten to the values of secularism, democracy and even values of moderate Islam. Being a secular democratic country, India always perceives Islamic fundamentalism and pan Islamism as threat to its long cherished political institutions and political integrity. India has been experiencing insurgency in the Kashmir valley inspired by Islamic fanaticism and pan Islamic fundamentalism. In Assam of Northeast India, Muslim United Liberation Front of Assam (MULTA), which is popularly believed to have proximity with many transnational Islamic fundamentalist groups, has launched its subversive activities in Assam and other parts of Northeast India.[17]

Bangladesh is predominantly a Muslim country. Besides recognizing Islam as the State's religions, the Constitution in its fundamental principles of State Policy, says, *"Absolute trust and faith in the Almighty Allah shall be the basis of all actions."*[18] How shall Bangladesh in its present institutional structure be treated? Is it a moderate Islamic or a theocratic State with religious conservatism?

To address this question, we need to look at the ideology and objectives of the major political parties of Bangladesh. The major political parties are-AL, BNP, Jatiyo Party (Ershad), Islamic United Front (IUF) and the Left parties (LPs) like Bangladesh Communist Party, Worker's Party etc. Among them, AL and LPs are socialist oriented and have faith in the politics of secularism and representative democracy based on socialism. Although AL has nation-wide influence, the LPs always remain marginalized and alienated in the politics of Bangladesh. AL introduced "socialism" and "secularism" in the guiding principles of the State. JP, headed by General Hossain Md. Ershad has leaning towards Islam. As a result, General Ershad, in an amendment of the constitution in June 1988, introduced Islam as the "State Religion" by discarding "socialism" and "secularism". The BNP has always maintained its closer proximity with Islam and therefore it has cordial relations with the fundamentalist groups. It entered into an electoral alliance with the fundamentalist groups in the General Election 2001 and formed a coalition government with IUF. As mentioned earlier, Bangladesh Army that perceives itself as the only force holding Bangladesh together is still a major force in the politics of the country. According to Dr. Subhash Kapila, *in term of socio-economic composition, the bulk of regular members of the Bangladesh's armed forces are drawn from the poor and economically backward rural areas*. Therefore, they are susceptible to Islamic fundamentalist influences and current day trends of pan Islamism in the Muslim world.[19] Besides, as stated above, most of the senior cadres of the Bangladesh armed forces share inter-personal relationships with the Pakistani Army. Needless to mention here, the bulk of Bangladesh's army members were initially recruited from the repatriated Bengali personnel of the Pakistani Army (East Bengal Regiment).

Therefore, it appears that the forces having faith in Islam and pan Islamism are more influential than the secular, socialist democratic forces in the politics of Bangladesh. They always reiterate and harbor anti-Indianism in their politics of national consolidation and perceive India as a big threat to the security and territorial integrity of Bangladesh and their position within Bangladesh's national politics. The AL believes that friendly relations with India are indispensable for better environment in South Asia. Such an environment is beneficial not only for the interests of the two countries, but also for the South Asia region as a whole.

There are many, who believe that Bangladesh is emerging as a major safe heaven for Islamic terrorist formations. According to Bertil Lintner, a revolution is taking place in Bangladesh that threatens the region and beyond if left unchallenged. Islamic fundamentalism, religious intolerance, militant Muslim groups with link to international terrorist groups, a powerful military with ties to the militants, the mushrooming of Islamic school churning out radical students, middle class apathy, poverty and lawlessness—all are combining to transform the nation.[20] Bangladesh Assessment Group on terrorism, in a report on terrorism in Bangladesh for the three quarters of 2003 also indicated about the existence of Al-Quada operatives in Bangladesh and its subversive activities in conjunction with the local Islamic groups.[21]

Their assessment cannot be ruled out. There have been spurts in the activities of the Islamic extremists in 2003. Some of the major incidents were [22]:

August 14: Police in Saudi Arabia arrested 22 terror suspects, including 11 Bangladeshis, from a house in the southern province of Jizan.

June 16: A Time Report in June 16, 2003 issue indicated that Islamic extremists of Bangladesh might be attempting to make a radioactive "dirty" bomb.

March 11: Police destroyed a training centre of the Islamic group Jamaat- ul-Mujahideen (JUM), Bangladesh in the Hujrapur area of Chapainawabganj district. Five cadres were arrested and manuals on "Jehad" were intercepted.

March 1: A police officer was killed and at least 10 others were injured in bomb blasts at the International Trade Fair in Khulna.

February 25: Police recovered 16 bombs from the residence of a religious leader, Maulana Fazlul Karim, in Charmonai, near Barisal, on the first day of an annual religious celebration.

February 13: At least seven powerful bombs were exploded in quick succession inside a house in Chholo Gurgola of Dinajpur town, leaving three persons injured. Police recovered huge arms, ammunitions, bomb-making chemicals, and a 'subscription' receipt of an annual Islamic group from the blast site.

January 17: At least eight persons were killed and eight others were wounded in bomb blasts at a carnival in Daniapur village, Tangail district. Harkat-ul-Jehadi-e-Islami, Bangladesh (HUJI-BD), which is believed to have link to the AL-Qaeda international terrorist network, is the prime suspect in instigating, planning, execution of all these incidents in conjunction with the JUM, its youth wing, the Arif Reza Commando Force (ARCF) and the Islamic Chhatra Shibir, the youth wing of Jamaat-e-Islami. HUJI-BD has now its branch offices in all the major divisional cities and districts including those of Chittagong, Cox's bazer, Shylet, Jessore, Brahmanbaria, Comilla. It also maintains altogether 19 training establishments scattered in different parts of the country.[23] Among them, Mohiursunnals madrassa, Baluchhera, Nayapara training establishments are located at Cox's Bazer district. The centre is famous for piracy, smuggling, arms dealings and gunrunning. It is the stronghold of the fundamentalist Jamaat-i-Islami and its youth wing Islamic Chhatra Shibir. The intensity of Islamization process in the CHT is also very high. We have noticed in the second chapter that between 1979 and 1984, approximately 20, 0000 to 40, 0000 socially, economically poor uneducated Muslims have been rehabilitated in the CHT. Fundamentalist groups with overt and covert backing of the military took advantage of mushrooming madrasa institutions to spread madrasa education to these socially and economically disadvantaged Bengali settlers. This resulted in gradual increase in the number of mosques and madrasa in the area. The following table will show how the number of mosques went on increasing in the CHT over the years:

Year	*Mosques*	*Madrasas*
1961	40	2
1974	200	20
1981	592	35

Source: Mohsin, *op.cit.* p. 179.

It shows that the number of mosques and madrasas gradually went on increasing in the CHT. According to the Peace Campaign Group (PCG),[24] there are more than 300 madrasas and mosques in the Khagrachari district alone.[25] Among the nineteen training establishments of the HUJI-BD, three of them are in the CHT, from which two are located in the Banderban district that has geographical proximity with Cox's Bazar and the other one is in the Rangamati district. Domestic and international Islamic NGOs like Bangladesh Islamic Foundation and Al Rabeta usually fund the madrasas and the mosques. They have renamed many places in the CHT with Islamic traditions. For instance, the main road of the Khagrachari district town was kept after Sahid Kader. Several places of Panchari, Diginala, Banderban have also been renamed with similar Islamic culture like Islampur, Mohammadpur etc. Beside these, many religious establishments of the Jummas were set ablaze, many Buddhist monks were beaten up and killed and many Jummas, especially women were forcibly converted into Islam. Religious persecution in the CHT has been accompanied with the following main features: [26]

i. Forcible conversion to Islam,

ii. Destruction of temples and churches,

iii. Prevention of worship.

i. Forcible conversion to Islam is another feature of Islamization process in the CHT. Whenever, the Bangladesh armed forces arrested any Jumma, it gave the option of either torture or conversion to Islam in order to escape inhuman torture. They also intimidated and encouraged the spread of Islamic missionary activities in the CHT. For instance, Al Rabita, an Islamic NGO has established its office in Langadu and Alikadam, remotest areas in the Rangamati and Banderban districts and working there under the intimidation of the security forces. It converted 17 Marma people (a traditional Buddhist community) to Islam at Alikadam in 2002.[27] Its charitable works are also strictly meant for the Muslims.

Religious persecution in the CHT has been accompanied by destruction of temples and churches. For instance, in 1986, the Bangladesh armed forces and the settlers destroyed the Boalkali temple, an orphanage centre, Dhalaina temple, Bagaichari Mukh temple, Pujgong temple. The army also destroyed the Betchari Christian church on 31 October 1990.

Another distressing feature is that there are violent attacks against worshippers, control over religious functions and traveling to sacred places. The military rule in the CHT once made it mandatory to take permission for celebration of religious festivals and visiting the sacred places in the CHT.[28]

After the peace accord, although the problem of religious persecution has been improved to some extent, the intensity of Islimization process has not declined. As stated in the second chapter, unofficial settlement of poor uneducated Muslim Bengalis from plain areas is still going on. Having faith in conservative form of Islam and madrasa education, these settlers do not also believe in family planning program. On the other hand, there is a tendency of emigration among a section of educated Jummas to foreign countries like Canada, France, the USA, Australia, New Zealand. Consequently, there is a declining trend in the percentage of Jumma population in the CHT's population.

What is most disturbing is the presence of HUJI-BD's training establishments in the CHT and voluntary rehabilitation and settlement of the Rohingya Muslim refugees (from Myammar) in the southern part of the Banderban district in close adjacent to the Cox's Bazer. A spread of HUJI-BD's network throughout the CHT shall bring severe physical repercussions on the life of the Jumma people in the CHT.[29]

Question is needed to be asked at this juncture of this part of dissertation – how does Islamic fundamentalism impinge on India's national security? There are many areas where India's national security remains at stake if these fundamentalist forces remain active in Bangladesh in general and the CHT in particular. *First,* their targets are the secular intellectuals , religious minority groups . Attack on the secular values is a great challenge to the preservation and promotion of secular credentials of Indian politics in India and South Asia region as a whole. Like the Pakistani regimes , they also hold the view that the Muslims are unsafe in India and it is their responsibility to help them liberated. Similarly, indiscriminate attacks on the minority communities develop the problem of forced (illegal) migration into Indian states like West Bengal, Tripura, Assam and Meghalaya. This , in return, generated communal tension and insurgency movement in Tripura, Assam Magalaya and Miroram. For instance, ethnic tension persists between Chakma vs. Mizo in Mizoram, Chakma and Hajong vs. Arunachalese in Arunachal Pradesh, Tribal, particularly Tripuri vs. Bengali in Tripura and Assamese vs. Bengali emigrants (both Hindu and Muslim) in Assam. *Secondly* , whenever, the fundamentalist forces remained in power in Bangladesh, they tried to develop friendly ties with India's strained neighbours . Such a development harms not only India's commercials interests in Bangladesh, but also becomes contrary to its geo-strategic interests in the region. *Thirdly,* since HUJI-BD is believed to have link to Al-Quaeda international terrorist network , its involvement in many terrorist attacks in India can not ruled out. For instance, the arrest of Aftab Ansari alias Farhan Malik, prime accused in the American Centre attack in Kolkatta, led to the disclosure regarding the international linkages between the Pakistan based Jaish-e-Mohammed (JeM), Lashkar-e-Toiba (LeT) and HUJI-Pak and HUJI-BD.[30] *Finally,* since these forces have absolute faith in Allah, they consider birth control as an insult to Islam. Therefore, it silently supports population explosion in the country. As a result, the trend in the growth rate of Bangladesh's population is very high. The poor economy of Bangladesh with such a situation further exacerbates the problem of Muslim illegal immigration/economic migration/voluntary migration in different parts of India.

Already the number of Muslim population along the Indo-Bangladesh border districts of Assam, Meghalaya, Tripura and West Bengal have increased. For instance, Dubri, (74.3%), Barpeta (59.4%), Hailakandi (57.7%), Goalpara (53.7%), Karimganj (52.3%) and Nogao (51%) are all Muslim majority districts of Assam. Muslims are going to be majority in the following districts of Assam-Marigao (47.6%), Bangaigao (38.5%), Kacher (36.1%), and Dorang (35.5%).[31] West Bengal is the third largest Muslim populated state in India with 25.2% of the total state's population. Like Assam, the border districts like Murshidabd (63.7%), Maldah (49.7%), Birbum (35.1%), North Dinajpur, (47.4%) have more Muslim population.[32] Similarly the Muslims constitute 15.2% of total population of the Garo Hills in Magalaya. [33] Muslims in Assam have already formed Muslim United Liberation Front (MULTA) for the liberation of the Muslims in the Northeast and West Bengal.

III

THE CHITTAGONG HILL TRACTS POLITICAL CRISIS AND REFUGEE INFLUX INTO INDIA

The CHT political crisis has generated refugee problem from time and again in India. In 1947, when the CHT was awarded to East Pakistan , many Jummas, mostly belonging to the Chakma community emigrated to Tripura and Lushai hills of present Mizoram state . But the exodus in large number took place in 1960's and 1980's. In the early 1960's , when the construction of the Kaptai dam uprooted 1,00,000 Jumma pepole, thousand of Chakmas took shelter in India. While some of the Chakma families settled down in Tripura and Assam, about 35,000 Chakmas were finally dispatched to Northeastern Frontier Agency (NEFA), now Arunachal Pradesh. About 86,000 Chakmas are living in different parts of Mizoram, particularly along the Indo-Bangladesh border areas. Some of them have been have been living there since pre-1947 days. But the Government of Mizoram alleges that many of them had migrated to the state from the CHT between 1979, 1982 and 1984.[34] When communal tension between the Jummas and the settlers occurred in 1979 and 1984, some Chakma, Tripura and Mog families moved into Tripura. However, very shortly, they were repatriated to the CHT. The largest exodus of refugees into Tripura from the CHT took place in the second half of 1980's, when between 1986 and 1989 more than fifty thousands Jummas became refugees following severe deterioration of the CHT's law and order situation. Repatriation of these refugees has been completed towards the end of 1997 following conclusion of an agreement between the Jumma Refugee Welfare Association (JRWA) and the GoB and an peace agreement between the PCJSS and the GoB.

How does the refugee exodus impinge on India's national security? There are many areas where this refugee influx created problems and brought negative repercussions on India's security. *First,* the refugee issue created ethnic tension between the refugees and the local inhabitants. It is noticeable in Arunachal Pradesh and Mizoram. The local inhabitants of Arunachal Pradesh and Mizoram attacked Chakma concentrations several times, torching down their houses and creating economic blockade against them. Hundreds of people, mostly the affected group, have been displaced in such communal violence in both the states. The Government of India had to deploy para-military forces in large numbers, whenever the situation turned worse. Tension between the local and the Chakmas cropped up mostly due spread of ethnic nationalism and the later's fear of demographic imbalance, competing economic interests etc.[35] *Secondly,* the refugee problem in Arunachal Pradesh and Mizoram has also emerged as an issue of irritant between the central and the state government. In Arunachal Pradesh, while the state government and All Arunachal Pradesh Student Union (AAPSU) vociferously opposed the move of granting the Chakmas and the Hajong refugees Indian citizenship in the state and issued 'quit' notices against them from time to time, the Central Government held the view that the Chakma and the Hajong refugees were eligible for Indian citizenship. In 1994, the Ministry of Home Affairs reiterated that since the Chakma and Hajong refugees of Aunachal Pradesh fulfilled *Section V of the Indian Citizenship Act of 1955,* they should be granted Indian citizenship.[36] On the contrary, people in Arunachal Pradesh (Changlang and Lohit districts) formed deportation committee to launch agitation for immediate deportation of the refugees from the state. The Supreme Court of India in its verdict on a Public Interest Litigation filed by the National Human Rights Commission (NHRC) ordered that the Chakmas and the Hajong refugees should not be removed from the state and directed the state government to secure the life and properties of the refugees and to take necessary step for registering the refugees as Indian citizens.[37] The core committee on refugee issue called an 11 hour strike on 22 January 1996 in protest against the Apex

Court's verdict. In Mizoram, while the state government alleges but without concrete evidence about the presence of illegal Chakma migrants, the Central Government denies it saying that if there are such elements, they should be identified. However, the state government failed to do so. Thirdly, although like Arunachal Pradesh and Mizoram, refugees who came to Tripura in 1980's did not create anti-refugee sentiment in Tripura, it created some uneasiness among the local people living nearby the refugee camps and the Government of India as well. The refugees with assured ration and relief in the camps together with business activities became economically better off than the locals. Employment opportunities for the locals have also been free zed with the refugees getting employed as cheap labor. It occasionally created social tension between the refugees and the local peoples.

It also created some security related problems to the Government of India. India under domestic and international pressure had to allow foreign dignitaries and activists of international human rights organizations to visit the refugee camps, although Tripura was not then open for foreigners due to security reasons. The Government of India was criticized when it refused permission to some of them. In 1996, the Unrepresented People's Organization (UNPO) was not permitted to visit the refugee camps. Fourthly; The Government of India spent near about Rs. 93 crores[38] for the refugees who came to Tripura in the 1980's alone till their last phase of repatriation. Although the amount was not big as compared to the UNHCR's role in refugee management, it was an extra economic burden for a developing a nation like India. Finally, illegal cross border movement of people created problem for the Indian Border Security Force (BSF) to keep strong vigilance along the Indo-Bangladesh border. Such illegal movement of people from the refugee camps across the border had also sometimes been accompanied with smuggling of goods and sensitive intoxicated materials like heroine, pensedyl etc.

Beside these, the CHT political crisis also stood always as one of the major irritants in the Indo-Bangladesh relations. Whenever, the issues like Farakka Water barrage, military rule in Bangladesh and its anti Indian foreign policy stood as irritants in Indo-Bangladesh relations, the CHT political crisis with India's indirect involvement in it further fueled tension and took the Indo-Bangladeshi relations at the lowest level. Medias in India and many intellectuals and human rights organizations criticized the GoB for fragrant human rights violations against the Jummas. The GoB always took such criticism negatively and blamed the Government of India for backing the PCJSS and SB and creating an uneasy political environment in the CHT.

Conclusion

From the above discussion and analysis, it appears that the CHT political crisis impinges on India's national security in many ways. In the 1960's and 1970's, the Mizo insurgency used the CHT as its main base in planning and execution of anti India activities. Through the CHT, it also established nexus with India's unfriendly nations and many international human rights organizations. Insurgency having cross border backing and closer proximity with the Sino-Pakistani military nexus even questioned about India's political and geographical integration of Northeast with the rest of India in 2nd half of 1960's and early 1970's. India could overcome such a challenge in the 1980's with China's termination of its relations with the Northeast insurgency following normalization of Sino-Indian relations. However, still insurgency continues to be a major problem for improving human security environment in the Northeast.

Besides standing as an irritant in Indo-Bangladesh relations, the CHT political crisis also generated refugee problem in Indian states. The maintenance of the refugee was not only an economic burden for the Government of India, but it also threatened communal harmony in Indian states like Arunachal Pradesh, Mizoram and even in Tripura to some extent.

The most worrying issue is the intensification of Islimization process in the CHT and the rise of Islamic fundamentalism throughout Bangladesh. It is the most challenging force for preserving and promoting Indian political values and security interests in South Asia. It generated the problem of forced migration among the Jummas in the CHT and other minority groups of Bangladesh into many Indian states creating social tension between the natives and the immigrants. It can also shake India's security fabric in conjunction with the international terrorist organizations. The proliferation Muslim population and madrasas along the eastern and Northeastern Indo-Bangladesh border and formation of MULTA in Assam are indicating factors in this connection.

So long as the CHT political crisis continues, it will continue to pose a threat to the security interests of India in all these respects because the CHT political crisis is linked to all these developments.

NOTES AND REFERENCES

1. Mr. Sainghaka, in an interview with Mr. Subhir Bhaumik, B.B.C. Eastern India Correspondent, as stated in Subhir Bhaumik, *Insurgent Crossfire: North East India*, Lancer Publishers: New Delhi, 1996, p. 147.
2. *Ibid.*, p. 163.
3. *Ibid.*
4. See, Secret, "*Extremist Camps in Bangladesh*", a report prepared by the Research and Analysis Wing (RAW) about the locations of the Northeast insurgent groups in Bangladesh. Also see, Subir Bhaumik, *The Troubled Periphery : Crisis of India's Northeast*, a forthcoming book to be published by Penguin. Also see, Jayanta Debnath, *Santrasklanta Tripura*, Danik Sambad Publishers, Agartala, 2001, p.304, Editorial Note of the *Statesman*, 30 November 2002, *The Hindustan Times*, New Delhi, 1 December 2002, p.1, *The Telegraph*, 12 May, 2003.
5. *Ibid.*
6. *Ibid.*
7. Also, see *http://www.tehelka.com/channels/currentaffairs/2002/mar/25/ca03250*, http://*www.satp.org/satporgtp/countries/bangladesh/*. It is also based on my interactions with some local Jummas of the CHT when I visited the Khagrachari district of the CHT in July 2003.
8. The coastal area stretching from the port city of Chittagong south through Cox's Bazer to the Burmese border is a notorious centre for piracy, smuggling, arms dealing and gun running. Last years several arms loaded trucks were intercepted in this area. To meet this argument, see, http://*www.asiapacificms.com/articles/bangladesh_terror/*. Also see, Sahorab Hassan, "Nana Sanggarche per Parbattya Chattagram Uttaptta Haye Uteche" (Different types of clashes have made the CHT unstable), in *Dainik Sambad*, Agartala, 19 March 2005.
9. H.D. Ghoshal et.al., *International Relations*, New Delhi, Unique Publishers, 2000, p. 770.
10. Jayanta Debnath, *Santrasklanta Tripura*, Dainik Sambad

Publishers: Agartala, 2001, p. 247.

11. The Government of India sheltered the PCJSS and its armed wing –Shanti Bahini in its territory. However, it never accepted this allegation, which came from Bangladesh. Instead it went on denying continuously. See Subir Bhaumik, op.cit., pp. 253-259. Also see Subir Bhaumik et. al. *Living on the Edge: Essays on the Chittagong Hill Tracts, Bangladesh*, South Asia Forum for Human Rights: Kathmandu, 1997, pp. 127-136.
12. For instance, when on 29 January 2003 India asked to handover its 88 wanted elements living illegally in Bangladesh, it denied the fact. Instead it handed over India a list of its wanted elements living in India including the names of some PCJSS members. Mr. Subir Bhaumik also told me about non repatriation of some prominent PCJSS members after the Peace accord of 1997 during a discussion with him about the matter in Kolkata in 2003.
13. See http:// ***www.saag.org/papers3/paper235.html***.
14. Based on my field trip and observation about the educational environment of the TTADC area of Tripura in June 2003.
15. For instance, the drop out rate (I-X) for the year 2001-2002 was 85.94%. See the booklet on drop out rate, published by the *Directorate of School Education*, Government of Tripura, 2003.
16. According to the 1991 population census of Tripura, out of 27,440827 population in the state, the tribal population constituted just 6,620703 (24.12%). *Statistical Department*, Government of Tripura.
17. http:// ***www.satp.org/satporgtp/countries/bangladesh/***.
18. Bangladesh Constitution: Part II Article 8 (I A).
19. Dr. Subhash Kapila on the nature of the Bangladesh armed forces and growth Islamic fundamentalism in http:// ***www.saag.org/papers3/paper235.html***.
20. Bertil Lintner on rising fundamentalism and religious intolerance in Bangladesh in http:// ***www.asiapacificms.com/articles/bangladesg_terror/***
21. Bangladesh Assessment 2003 in ***http://www.satp.org/satporgtp/countries/bangladesh/***
22. *Ibid.*
23. Suman K. Chakraborty, 'Terror's New Home", *India Today*, December 9, 2002, pp. 52-53.
24. Peace Campaign Group (PCG) is a Delhi based human rights organization.

25. See the report of the post accord situation of the CHT, prepared by the PCG, 10 April 2002, p. 13.
26. For detail on religious persecution against the Jummas in the CHT, see http:// *www.anglefire.com/ab/jumma.religion.html*
27. *Ibid.*
28. *Ibid.*
29. For details about the HUJI-BD network in Bangladesh, see the map which was published in *India Today,* December 9, 2002, p. 53. Also see, Secret, "*The Extremist Camps in Bangladesh*" a report prepared by RAW on HUJI-BD's network in Bangladesh including the CHT.
30. http:// *www.satp.org/satporgtp/countries/bangladesh/*
31. Manik Rao Hotlia Gavit, Deputy Minister in the Home affairs, Government of India in reply to a question raised by C. Ramchadraar, Member of Parliament, Rajya Sabha about the increased in Muslim population told the House about the number of Muslim population in West Bengal and Northeast India, *The Rajya Sabha Session,* 18 March 2005. Also see Manas Biswas, "Muslim Janasangkar Anupatil Hare Pratam Laksha Deep, Ditio Jumma Kashmir, Tritia Assam, Chaturtha West Bengal: Sangsadee Mantrir Tattyo," in *Syandan Patrika,* Agartala, 19 March 2005, p. 2.
32. *Ibid.*
33. *Ibid.*
34. Saradindu Mukerji, *Subjects, Citizens and Refugees: Tragedy in the Chittagong Hill tracts* (1947-1998) Indian Centre for the Study of Forced Migration: New Delhi, 2000, p. 108.
35. *Ibid.*
36. *Ibid.*, p. 88.
37. *Ibid.*, p. 92.
38. Based on the statistical data provided by the *Department of Relief and Rehabilitation*, Government of Tripura.

4

The Chittagong Hill Tracts Political Crisis and the Government of India Policy

As stated in the introduction that the pro-Indian attitude of the Jummas during partition, their ethnic and cultural linkages with the communities of many North-eastern Indian states, CHT's geographical proximity with Mizoram and Tripura and refugee influx into India from the CHT made India indirectly involved in the CHT political crisis. Therefore, the Government of India had to adopt a policy to deal with the challenges, which are emanated from the CHT political crisis.

This chapter would attempt to deal with the Government of India's policy in the CHT for the last five decades. While analyzing this, the chapter would primarily argue that India paid more attention to its geo-strategic, political, and economic interests because the intensity of threat posed by the CHT political crisis was low. It did not shake the fabric of India's national security at a wider extent.

Geo-Strategic Interests

Geo-strategic location of a place is an important factor for determining its national and international importance. Tibet being in high altitude, India and China recognizes the importance of its geo-strategic location particularly in time of conventional warfare between the two 'hostile'[1] neighbors. Strategically, the Chinese PLA remains always in a more advantageous position than the Indian armed forces for their position in Tibet being comparatively in high altitude. This was found in the 1962 Sino-Indian border war and other occasional border skirmish between the Chinese and the Indian armed forces. The availability of natural and human resources also determines the importance of a place.

In our early discussion and analysis, we have noticed that the rules of the 'Two Nation Theory' justified natural merger of the CHT with the Union of India in 1947. Contemporary Jumma leaders (mentioned earlier) hoisted Indian National Flag and campaigned for its merger with India. However, the national leaders of then India did not pay much attention to make the CHT politically and geographically integrated with independent India. On the other hand, despite accession of Junagadh and Kashmir proved to be a source of considerable contention, the Government of India paid its best possible attention towards the two Princely states. The difference in Government of India's attention towards the CHT and the two Princely states can be understood through a comparative analysis on geo-strategic location of these three regions and their importance for India's national security interests.

The geographical location of the CHT did not serve any national security interests for India at the time of partition as compared to Junagadh and Kashmir. The CHT being located in the extreme Northeast from the mainland India, it did not have direct physical contiguity with the non-Muslim populated areas of Bengal. Cox's Bazaer, a coastal town, was also not included within the physical boundary of the CHT.

Junagadh, a princely state, was located on the West Coast of India having contiguous border. Though the state had a Muslim ruler, it was predominantly a Hindu populated state with 82%[2] of the total population. The Government of India, in the light of its geographical location and its large Hindu population wanted to make it integrated with Indian Union. Kashmir was important to India for different reasons. Though Kashmir was overwhelmingly a Muslim populated state, it had also substantial Hindu and Buddhist population. Its Maharaja was a Hindu by religion. National Conference (NC), the then largest represented political party in the state was socialist and secular in nature and its leader Sheik Abdullah had good relations with Nehru.[3] Geographically it is also contiguous to India and is in high altitude. The Government of India naturally realized its importance not only for protecting the interests of the non-Muslim population, but also because of its geo-strategic location.[4] Kashmir's integration was also important for India in order to falsify the theory of the creation of Pakistani State as well as to promote and strengthen its secular credentials.[5]

Political Interests

Although the geographical location of the CHT did not serve the national security interests in 1947, the CHT and its people appeared to be important for the Government of India in the later years. After the Naga insurgency, the Mizos also began armed struggle against Indian rule for freedom in the Mizo hills. The CHT emerged as their main training center and base for conducting all subversive operations against the Indian security forces deployed there. The Government of India realized the importance of the Jummas and used them as strategic pawns against the Indian rebel groups. According to Subir Bhaumik, the Jummas of the CHT always served, as 'strategic pawn' for the Government of India in meeting its political interests.[6] Mr. Bhaumik's observation about the Government of India's policy towards the CHT and its people is true on many grounds.

In the early 1970s, the Mizo rebellion in the Mizo hills reached at its peak with fresh recruitment of Mizo youths and training facilities and arms supply provided to them by Pakistan. The CHT, being geographically contiguous to the Mizo hills, the insurgents carried on their operations from across the border very successfully. Human security environment had severely been deteriorated with virtual decline in the law and order situation in the entire region because of the failure of the security forces to contain further escalation of the crisis. At this critical juncture, Mrs. Indira Gandhi, the then Prime Minister of India, under the advice of Field Marshal General Maneck Shaw, adopted a strategy of backing the Chakmas living on both sides of the border against the Mizos. Given the historical animosity between the two communities[7]. General Shaw was convinced that the Chakmas could be used as human shield and their resources could be utilized against the Mizo insurgency movement.[8] The immediate step was the creation of the Chakma Autonomous District Council (CADC) in 1971 to secure the confidence of the Chakmas. The Chakmas also wholeheartedly co-operated with the Indian agencies to contain the Mizo insurgency. The Mizo insurgent leaders in severe reaction to this also declared a price reward of Rs.3 lakhs for the head of Mr. Sura Krishna Chakma for his mastermind role in the emergence of a holly alliance between the Chakmas and the Indian security agencies. The Mizo rebels along with the Pakistani armed forces also butchered Chakmas several times. For instance, the Mizo rebels in retaliation of the Chakmas' co-operation with the Indian army perpetrated the Bhusanchara massacre in the CHT in 1971.

In the post independent period of Bangladesh, the Jumma leaders thought that the Government of India would create pressure on the Government of newly independent Bangladesh to establish political autonomy for the Jummas. Rajmata Binita Roy and Mukur Kanti Khisa (a retired Indian Chakma diplomat) approached Mrs. Gandhi and requested her to see the rights of the Jummas be protected and promoted in the independent Bangladesh.[9] However, Mrs.Gandhi did not pay any importance to their appeal. Instead, she paid more attention to India's national security interests. *First,* Sheik Mujibur Rahman, the founding leader of Bangladesh pledged not to allow any Indian rebel group operating against India from its soil. *Secondly,* immediately after Bangladesh emerged as independent entity, India and Bangladesh signed a long twenty years treaty of 'peace, friendship and co-operation'. Implementation of the treaty was important for meeting the concerns of India's national security interests. There were many anti Mujib elements (Purba Bangla Communist Party, some repatriated army officers from the Pakistani army) who did not welcome conclusion of such a treaty. Mrs. Gandhi was naturally convinced that any move of creating extra pressure on Mujib at a time when he was attempting to consolidate his political position in the country would be counterproductive and contrary to India's national interests.

The assassination of Mujib in August 1975 and a change in regime in Bangladesh changed the whole scenario. The post Mujib's regime decided to withdraw from the treaty signed earlier. It also developed friendly ties with India's hostile neighbors and Washington-Beijing-Islamabad Cold War axis. It was at that critical juncture of India and Bangladesh relations, the Jummas of the CHT reappeared to be important the Government of India. According to Mr. Gopal Chakma,[10] the Government of India directed the RAW officials of Agartala to immediately establish link with the PCJSS and the leaders of its armed wing Shanti Bahini (SB).[11] From 1975 onwards, the Indian agencies not only trained several batches of the rebel fighters but also liaised and transferred weapons and funds regularly to the rebels.[12] The policy had dual objectives in mind–to use the SB fighters against the Mizo insurgency (reopened their bases in the CHT after friendly regime came to power following Mujib's assassination) and to put extra diplomatic pressure on the GoB to change its anti India rhetoric.

Although, the policy failed to meet the second objective, it produced desired result for the first objective. For instance, on 4 December 1976, a large SB squad attacked an MNF "transit camp" at Rangkhyang Bhoga near Bilaichari in the CHT and killed 12 MNF guerillas.[13]

In 1986, following severe deterioration of the CHT law and order situation, there was a large exodus of Jumma refugee into Tripura. The Government of India provided rations to them until the last phase of their repatriation in 1997. India's press and media occasionally highlighted about the traumatic plight of the Jummas. However, the Government of India remained within its limits. Although it favored an honourous settlement of the refugee imbroglio, it did not want to infuriate the GoB by making the CHT political crisis much highlighted and internationalized. For the purpose, instead of allowing the UNHCR to play its role, it kept the refugees within its administrative jurisdiction. The Government of India also justified seeking the opinion from the GoB while allowing any international commission to visit the refugee camps. For instance, it permitted the CHT Commission to visit the refugee camps in 1990 only after the GoB allowed it to visit the CHT. Similarly, it refused permission to the UNPO when the GoB did not allow the organization to visit the CHT in 1996.

The PCJSS started negotiations with the GoB following democratic election in 1996. However, it is opined that although negotiations produced no meaningful result, the PCJSS had to continue the process of negotiations under Government of India's pressure.[14] Similarly, the Government of India created pressure on the refugee leaders to continue negotiations with GoB to finalize repatriation of the refugees. [15] Mr. Ramesh Bhandari, the then Governor of Tripura , on the other hand, was overwhelmed with Dhaka's goodwill and generosity when he visited Bangladesh for sorting out the differences between the refugee leaders and the GoB in 1996. On his return he criticized the refugee leaders, saying that the situation in the CHT was quite conducive for repatriation.[16] Charges and counter charges between the refugee leaders and Mr. Bhandari created a controversy in the refugee repatriation process. The immediate result of that controversy was delay in rationing facilities to the refugees. In 1994, the Government of Tripura complained about non-release of Rs. 4.35 crores for maintenance of the refugees.[17] The CHT political crisis received the lowest priority in the Indian policy under the United Front (UF) government that emphasized on improving India's relations with all neighbours. "Gujaral Doctrine" of India's foreign policy was an indicative in this regard.

Real politick as an abiding feature in India's policy towards the CHT became more dominating in the 1990's because it paid more attention to its preferred political interests. *First,* the Government noticed that the anti Ershad demonstration and people's love for democracy in Bangladesh was reaching at peak. Therefore, the Government of India waited and observed the new developments in Bangladesh in the second half of 1980s. Excessive highlight of the refugee issue might be obstacle for developing better ties with the post Ershad's regime in Bangladesh. Moreover, since the conclusion of the Shimla accord between

India and Pakistan in 1975, the Government of India has been favoring bilateral solutions of all disputes and always stood against internationalization of such bilateral problem. *Secondly,* Government of India put pressure on the PCJSS and the refugee leaders mainly for its calculation that the AL, which is traditionally friendly to India, might come to power. Such a development would help India to revive the traditional bilateral friendly relations between the two countries. The calculation was correct as AL came to power in 1996. After AL came to power, India naturally intensified its pressure on the PCJSS and refugee leaders as relations between the two countries became friendly within a short time. The Government of India did not want to see the refugee crisis to be an irritant in improvement of India and Bangladesh relations. *Thirdly,* in 1997, both India and Bangladesh pledged to galvanize their bilateral co-operation in security arena and decided to counter cross border insurgency in the Northeast. The Government of India, in a reciprocal move, was obliged to delink its relations with the PCJSS movement. *Fourthly,* from the earlier experiences, the Government of India learnt that whenever bilateral relations between the two countries deteriorated, the GoB developed friendly ties with India's strained neighbors that introduced a new challenge for preserving her 'status qua' position in South Asia. It happened in the 1970s when the presence of Washington-Beijing-Islamabad Cold War axis's influence in Bangladesh worried the security policy makers of India. *Finally,* in the era of regionalism and globalization, the Government of India believed that harmonious relations with all the SAARC countries would help this regional economic arrangement moving forward. Bangladesh being the third largest economy and third influential actor (after India and Pakistan) in South Asia, its role in making the SAARC a successful organization was indispensable.

Economic Interests

Previous analysis has shown that the GoB has failed to meet its obligation on cross border insurgency. The Government of Tripura and Assam brought before the Central Government several times about the presence of Northeast rebel groups in the CHT and other parts of Bangladesh. The Government of Tripura even called for Interpol's assistance to apprehend the rebel leaders living in Bangladesh. However, until now the Central Government did not put enough diplomatic pressure on the GoB for sheltering the Northeast rebel groups. Naturally, question arises-why did the Government of India did not take up the issue seriously with its Bangladeshi counterpart?

In the early 1990s, the Government of India liberalized its economy with the introduction of 'New Economic Policy'. Bangladesh also greatly liberalized its trade regime. Bangladesh being the third largest economy in South Asia, the Indian companies were quick to take the advantage. As a result, very soon, the Indian goods flooded the Bangladesh's market. Besides exporting cosmetic products, Bangladesh's market has also been flooded with India's ceramics, dresses and medicines. The trend in Indo-Bangladesh trade relations remained always in favour of India over the years. While the Government of India exports goods to Bangladesh for nearly US $1.2 billions every year, Bangladesh export figure reaches just at US $ 100 millions.[18] Bangladesh's trade deficit against India between 1996 and 2001 was Tk. 25880 crores and 28 lakhs.[19] According to the Ministry of Commerce of Bangladesh, Bangladesh enjoys US $ 1 billion trade deficit against India every year.[20]

Apart from flooding Bangladesh's market with goods, India has also specific interests in Bangladesh's gas sector. Bangladesh has large reserve of natural gas, well in excess of its requirement. The Gas Authority of India (GAIL), Indian Oil Corporation (IOC) and Oil and Natural Gas Corporation (ONGC) have shown their interests for setting up a gas pipeline of nearly 300 kms long for benefiting especially the Northeast India.[21] The Central Government has already approved the proposal. Unocal, US oil giant also set forth US $ 1.2 billion Natural Gas Pipeline Project with a construction of 1,365 kms distance reaching up to New Delhi from the Northeast Bangladsh.[22] There is also speculation about laying a gas pipeline under the Bay of Bengal to help India gets an access to the sizeable gas reserves of Myanmar.

Bangladesh's software units also look for India's help. It needs coal and limestone for its industries. Meghalaya is an important destination for meeting Bangladesh these raw materials. Northeastern states also economically benefit through promotion of border trade. Items like oranges, pineapples, apples; grapes, floriculture products including orchid's medicinal plants, coal, limestone, and petroleum-based products from the region have lots of prospect through promotion of border trade. The region also benefits if Bangladesh permits transit and transshipment of

Indian goods. The Government of India is convinced that only harmonious bilateral relations between the two countries provide India a better access to all these economic facilities in Bangladesh.

It appears that the Government of India treats the Northeast insurgency as a local problem, which the state government can effectively deal with. Unlike the separatist movement in Kashmir, insurgency in the Northeast no more threatens about India's territorial integration. The Government of India also seems to believe that the situation in the region can remarkably improve once the economy in the region starts progressing. Northeast being geographically isolated from the mainland India and having long boundary with Bangladesh, better economic ties with Bangladesh and subsequent promotion of border trade can be an effective instrument for meeting this objective.

Conclusion

From the above analysis, it is clear that during the time of partition, the Government of India was moved more by geo-strategic calculation. As a result, CHT's geographical location and its non-important for meeting India's security concerns failed to draw the attention of the Indian national leaders. On the other hand, Kashmir and Junagadh being located on the western side of India having contiguous border were much important for meeting India's immediate security concerns. In the entire Nehruvian period, the CHT and its people remained neglected in India's security priority. Instead of raising any voice against gross human rights violations against the Jummas, the Government of India rather cordially welcomed the refugee exodus from the CHT and settled them in present Arunachal Pradesh of India.

The CHT and its people appeared to be important for India in 1970s also mainly for political reasons. To meet its national security interests, it created the CADC in present Mizoram state. The Government of India also backed the PCJSS following deterioration of Bangladesh in the post Mujib era. In the second half of 1980s, the Government of India mainly observed the developments of Bangladesh and based on this, it made political move. The new developments in Bangladesh urged India not to highlight much the refugee issue so that it did not stand as an irritant in cultivating better ties with a new Bangladesh. In the 1990s, following democratic elections, liberalization in trade regime in India and Bangladesh, Government of India looked for the newly emerged economic opportunities in Bangladesh. Its greater economic interests urged India to put excessive pressure on the PCJSS and the refugee leaders to find out an early solution of the CHT problem. Eight years have already been passed since the conclusion of the peace accord, however, it yet to be implemented. Rather the situation there has turned out to be more precarious (See second chapter). If this continues, there is every possibility of another refugee influx into India in a near future. However, the Government of India did not take the issue seriously because of its greater national interests.

Similarly, the Government of India knows well and has concrete evidence about the presence of Northeast rebel groups in Bangladesh, but its greater national interests in Bangladesh forbid India to show serious reaction. Its economic interests are more important than the rebel's presence in Bangladesh. Besides, economic prosperity in the Northeast depends on better economic ties and promotion of border trade with Bangladesh is an important aspect in this regard. For all these reasons, the Government of India went on ignoring the threat posed by the Northeast insurgency and the CHT political crisis.

NOTES AND REFERENCES

1. Until the visit of Rajiv Gandhi to China in 1988, relations between the two countries remained more or less strained. Although following the formation of Joint Working Group (JWG) on the existing border problem, tensions between the two countries have substantially been reduced; they are yet to find out a solution of the border dispute, which if remains so may make their relations again tensed.
2. Sumit Ganguly, *The Origin of War in South Asia: Indo-Pakistani Conflict Since 1947*, Vision Books: New Delhi, 1999, p. 32.
3. *Ibid.*, p. 35.
4. *Ibid.*, p. 41.
5. *Ibid.*, p. 39.
6. Subir Bhaumik, "Strategic Pawn: Indian Policy in the Chittagong Hill Tracts," in Subir Bhaumik et. al, *Living on the Edge: Essays on the Chittagong Hill Tracts*, South Asia Forum for Human Rights: Kathmandu, 1997, pp. 127-136.
7. Historically Chakmas and the Mizos are two antagonist communities against each other. This animosity made them fighting against each other several times.
8. Based on my interactions and interviews with some prominent Chakma leaders of Mizoram and Tripura. Their names have not been disclosed because they have requested the scholar to do so.
9. My interactions with Mukur Khanti Kisha at Rajghat Buddha Mandir premise in 2003.
10. Mr. Gopal Chakma is a retired officer of RAW, the intelligent agency of Government of India for External Affairs.
11. Based on my interactions with Mr. Gopal Chakma in Kolkata in 1998 and Agartala 2001.
12. Bhaumik et.al, *op. cit.*, p. 132. Also see Subir Bhuamik,

Insurgent Crossfire: Northeast India, Lancer Publishers: New Delhi, 1996, pp. 270-74.

13. *Ibid.*, p. 274.
14. Bhuamik *et. al*, *op. cit.* p. 133.
15. In February and July 1994, 1,228 families comprising 5,186 members were repatriated to Bangladesh. However, the next phase of repatriation was postponed repeatedly due to refusal of the refugees to return to the CHT unless the repatriated refugees were repatriated properly. Mr. Upendralal Chakma, the refugee leader, who along with a team visited the CHT, affirmed that the situation was not conducive for return due non-implementation of the 16 point package deal signed earlier in Tripura by the refugee leaders and the GoB's representatives. He stated that the repatriation process would not resume so long as the Government of Inaia did not properly rehabilitate the returnee refugees. For details see Saradendu Mukerji, *Subjects, Citizens and Refugees: Tragedy in the Chittagong Hill Tracts (1947-1998)*, Indian Centre for the Study of Forced Migration: New Delhi, 2000, pp. 106-107.
16. *Ibid.*
17. *Ibid.*. p. 108.
18. Abu Ahmed, " Bharatear Sathe Banijya Alochanar Strategy Paribatan Ana Uchit" (it is necessary to bring a change in strategy of trade relations with India), *Bhorer Kagaj*, a leading Bengali daily of Bangladesh, Dhaka, 20 May 2002.
19. Amir K. Md. Chowdhury, the Commerce Minister of Bangladesh told the Bangladesh National Assembly in response to a question on trade imbalance between India and Bangladesh. *The Dainik Sangram*, Dhaka, 1 April, 2002.
20. *Ibid.*
21. *Ajker Kagaj*, 27 June, 2002.
22. *The Statesman*, 1 November, 2001.

5

Conclusion

The study dealt with various dimensions of security including the national interests and security policy of India in the first section. It observed that although non-military dimension of security is being widely discussed at academic and foreign policy making level, traditional security with its mutual distrust, apprehension and suspicion continued to dominate the behaviour of the nation states in the domain of international relations in the beginning of the 21st century. The nation states continued to enhance their military strike capabilities at both conventional and nuclear level. The most powerful states are reluctant to implement various arms control, arms reduction treaties, and reduce nuclear stockpiles unconditionally. Therefore, in such a traditional security dilemma, in India too, the study has observed the realist school of thought to dominate and influence in the foreign policy making process. India's continuous researches in the ballistic missile development programs are enough empirical evidences in this connection. However, the study argued that the realists' understanding of security defining in term of national interests could not provide comprehensive security for all sections of society, because it most cases, interalia, it favoured the interests of the dominant groups, the interests of the non dominant groups remained ignored and neglected.

The second chapter dealt with the CHT political crisis and political movement of the Jummas. It observed that political and geographical integration of the CHT with Pakistan in 1947 crated a political crisis in the CHT, because the decision went against the political aspirations of the hill people in the CHT. The problem had been deteriorated in the post independent period of Bangladesh due to the rise of ethnic insurgency against the decision of the government of Bangladesh in militarization and implantation of Muslim Bengali settlers in the CHT.

A peace accord was signed between the Government of Bangladesh and the PCJSS on 2 December 1997 to establish peace and political stability in the CHT. However, patricidal killings amongst the Jummas and continued unofficial settlements of the Bengali settlers in the CHT made post accord the political environment more volatile and explosive in nature. In other words, the problem continued to be a major problem.

The third chapter studied the impact of the CHT political crisis on India's national security. It observed that the CHT being geographically contiguous to the Northeast India, its political crisis continued to impinge on India's national security in many areas, more particularly in the socio economic lives in the Northeast India. However, the treat posed by the CHT political crisis was not a formidable problem for India, because it did not pose an immediate threat to the greater security interests of India. Therefore, instead of firmly dealing with it, it rather favoured to pursue its preferred political, economic and other geo-strategic interests in the context of normal bilateral relations between India and Bangladesh.

As noted above, the realists continue to dominate the foreign policy making process in India. However, unlike the traditional realists, the realists in India assume 'security' as an interdependence concept, if not in global, at-least in South Asian context. Yet, their idea of interdependence in South Asian security is also much narrower as they include only China, India and Pakistan within the circle of interdependence paradigm of security. This means to say that they consider the behavior of China and Pakistan as the major source of threat to India's national security interests in South Asia. As a result, India reacted vociferously whenever China attempted to expand its influence in South Asian politics. India's reaction against the alleged Sino-Pakistani strategic cooperation was high because it perceived such cooperation as great threat to its national security interests and status quo in South Asia. India had also been worried about unabated cross-border terrorism in the Kashmir valley. The intensity of India's national and international propaganda warfare against cross-border terrorism in its Western sector was so high that it appeared that India's foreign policy once had become very much Kashmir and Pakistan centered.

The Eastern and Northeastern India also faces similar problem. The Government of India was and is well aware about growing infiltration of international terrorist elements, rise of Pan Islamism in Bangladesh and proliferation of Madrasa institutions along the India-Bangladesh border. The Tripura Government brought from time to time before the knowledge of the Central Government about the presence of several base camps of Northeast insurgent groups in Bangladesh. However, the Government of India never took these issues with GoB seriously for its greater economic and political interests present in Bangladesh. Instead, by treating Northeast insurgency as local problem, the Government of India emphasized more on economic progress of the region, for it believes; economic development in the region can preempt and bring down substantially the problem of insurgency. Therefore, the government of India preferred better economic ties and promotion of border trade with Bangladesh because of geographical isolation of the Northeast with the mainland India.

It is of-course undeniable that economic marginalization of the indigenous inhabitants is an important factor for the rise and escalation of ethnic nationalism and insurgency in many parts of Northeast. The outbreak of 'rat famine' in the Mizo hills in the late 1950's and alleged inadequate assistance from the Union and State (Assam) governments were some of the important factors, which led to the rise of Mizo nationalism and Mizo insurgency in the Mizo hills.[1] Similarly, economic deprivation and annihilation of the Tripura's tribal communities has been a major factor for the growth of tribal insurgency in the state. However, study of Northeast insurgency shall remain incomplete and be one-dimensional if one considers only the economic factor. A comprehensive study about

Northeast insurgency always requires looking at the problem of illegal immigration and trans- border movement of people from across the border (Bangladesh) into the region. Illegal immigration might not have eroded communal harmony in West Bengal [2], but it had been the main factor for the rise and escalation of low intensity conflicts in Assam, Meghalaya, Tripura and Arunachal Pradesh.[3]

It appeared in our analysis that there had been a serious discrepancy in India's approach of dealing with the problem. While it identified the Muslims as illegal immigrants, it treated the other minority groups of Bangladesh, particularly Hindus as refugees. During an operation against illegal immigration in 2003 along the India- Bangladesh border of West Bengal, the persons identified and arrested, as illegal immigrants were all Muslims. Why is there such discrepancy in India's policy of dealing with illegal immigration from Bangladesh? Of-course, increase in Muslim population along India-Bangladesh border has been a worrying factor for India's security. Over the years, most of the terrorists arrested in connection with various deadliest terrorist activities in India were Muslims. Hence, special attention deserved for the Muslim illegal immigrants. However, how long should India remain lenient towards the non-Muslim refugees (also illegal immigrants) from Bangladesh?

The biggest problem that India faces in this connection is identification of the immigrants (refugees). The repatriation of the Jumma (Chakma as the Medias called) refugees from South Tripura's refugee camps had been possible in 1997 because of their official record in the Refugee Registration Register and their voluntary willingness to be repatriated to the CHT. However, contrary to them, the Hindu refugees have neither any such official record nor any voluntary intention to return to Bangladesh. The more important is that most of them have already possessed valid legal documents (Ration Card, Voter Identity Card etc.) to challenge any move of depriving their Indian nationality. Naturally, question arises as to how far the Government of India will be successful in its attempt to counter the challenge of illegal immigration by providing Multiple National Identity Card (MNIC) [4] to its citizens.

However, students of tribal communities of the Northeast have different opinion. Some of them [5] opine that the Government of India, most cases, seemed to believe that its security interests were better served with the concentration of the refugees because of their more emotional and psychological attachment with mainstream Indian culture than the tribal communities who have more physical, cultural proximity with the people of South East Asia. For this reason as they opine, the India's approach has been lenient towards the Hindu refugees in the region. Discrepancy in the immigration policy is one aspect; another is the Government of India to put assailable diplomatic pressure on the GoB to stop sheltering the Northeast insurgents groups for its larger political and economic interests in the context of cordial bilateral relations. This leads naturally to ask a question— Is India against its citizens in the region?

The Fundamental Rights and Directive Principles of State Policy under Part IV of the Constitution direct the union and the state governments to ensure the rights of its citizens, protect and promote their interests in all possible ways. The idea of justice as laid down in this part of the constitution shall remain meaningless and unfruitful for its citizens in the region unless their concerns are seriously addressed and human security environment in the region is not improved in the coming years. Now what is desirable from the part of the Government of India to attain this objective?

There are many [6] who argue that the Government of India needs to adopt such policy that can help decimating the feeling of xenophobia from many indigenous communities of the region. For the purpose, it requires removal of the existing flaws in India's illegal immigration policy. This does not however mean that India should not shelter refugees at all. However, there shall be ways to repatriate them once the situation improves there. *Secondly,* The Government of India requires being very clear in its CHT policy and removes suspicion from the Bangladesh's security establishment about its alleged involvement in the CHT affairs, one of the many factors that has encouraged the Bangladesh's security establishment to back the Northeast insurgency. Once this is done, it can be an effective diplomatic tool to put pressure on the Government of Bangladesh to stop cross border insurgency in India's Northeast.

However, the question is –are these steps enough to counter and bring down insurgency in the Northeast? The objective of dismantling the infrastructure of the Northeast insurgency in Bangladesh may be achieved with India's effective diplomacy. However, experiences show that insurgency has continued unabated in Assam, Manipur, Nagaland even after "Operation Flush Out" in Bhutan in 2003 and several Indo-Burmese joint military operations along the Indo Burmese border over the years.

Therefore, we need to find out the root causes behind the rise and escalation of ethnic insurgency, ethnicism in the region. Illegal migration is one of such causes, which encouraged the rise of and escalation of low intensity conflicts in many parts of the Northeast, particularly in Assam, Meghalaya and Tripura. Simultaneously, we also need to find out the reasons, which generate illegal migration from Bangladesh in India. The illegal migration from the Muslim community of Bangladesh is voluntary in nature. They immigrate to India mostly for economic reasons. On the other hand, the minority communities of Bangladesh, particularly the Hindus immigrate to India due to fear of political and religion persecution. Therefore, in the case of minority communities, silent migration cannot be effectively countered so long as the security of the minority communities of Bangladesh is not improved. In other words, the ultimate trouble of destination lies not in India but in Bangladesh. The prospects of India's Northeast highly depend on a solution of this problem.

Now, what is most desirable from the Government of India to achieve this goal? In our previous analysis, we have seen that the rise of Islamic fundamentalism, influence of the military in the decision making process, lack of religious tolerance in Bangladesh are the main factors that threaten India's security. So, should India directly interfere in the politics of Bangladesh to counter the security threat posed by its (Bangladesh) political system? India's status as the most powerful nation in South Asia (when China is excluded from it) may be unquestionable. However, despite that, this strategy does not suit India because it brings more counter productive repercussions on India's security in South Asia. Israel can employ such a policy due to covert US's backing in its anti Palestinian operations. The US can employ 'Just War Theory' [7] because of being the most powerful state at the present international systemic structure. Moreover, like the US, India does not have enough military, economic and diplomatic power to deal with post war situation. Even the US had devastating experience in Vietnam and is facing a formidable challenge from the Iraqi insurgents in the post war period.

Institutional transformation does not come at random other than forceful imposition. Violence continues as people generally oppose such unlawful imposition of a regime by a foreign power. Iraq is now a classic example. Therefore, instead of going for that, India can rather prefer constructive engagement with the regimes of Bangladesh. The more the relations between the two countries are widened, the more it will be better for India as it can help not only promoting her interests but also to checkmate the anti secular and anti democratic forces in Bangladesh.

Of course, political system of Bangladesh is not responsible alone. The unraveling lenient of the India's illegal immigration policy towards the Hindus, corruption in the local administration, and electoral politics of the political parties with the immigrants equally encourage illegal immigration from across the border. These malpractices shall have to be stopped for greater interests of the country.

Once, Bangladesh is transformed into a liberal democratic country with institutional safeguards for the minority communities, the problem of forced migration and refugee influx into India from Bangladesh, and more particularly from the CHT shall remarkably come down. Our discussion and analysis in the second chapter felt the necessity of such institutional transformation for solution of the CHT political crisis. This means, security threat emanating from the CHT political crisis can be checkmated with such institutional transformation in Bangladesh. A decline in illegal immigration in the Northeast can also lessen the feeling of xenophobia present among many indigenous communities of Northeast, a condition that is most vital for bringing down insurgency in the region.

If this is happened, the two countries can also take some join initiatives for socio-economic upliftment of the disadvantaged communities living on both sides of the border. Border trade can be promoted by opening more Land Custom Service (LCS)[7] to reach modern market facilities to these disadvantaged groups.

NOTES AND REFERENCES

1. Subir Bhaumik, *Insurgent Crossfire: Northeast India,* Lancer Publishers: New Delhi, 1996, pp.142-143.
2. Illegal immigrants from Bangladesh are mostly Bengalis. Hence, by virtue of their belonging to the same community with similar culture and tradition, the problem of illegal immigration did not fuel much communal tension in West Bengal as happened in the Northeast.
3. Apart from the presence of the Chakma and Hajong refugees,

who settled in the early 1960,s, the Government of Arunachal Pradesh alleges that there are near about 35,000 Bangladeshi illegal immigrants in the state. See Saradindu Mukherji, *Subjects, Citizens and Refugees: Tragedy in the Chittagong Hill Tracts (1947-1998)*, Indian Center for the Study of Forced Migration: New Delhi, 2000, p.95.

4. Multiple National Identity Card (MNIC) is a pilot project launched by the Government of India. Its objectives are *(i)* to provide national identity cards to its citizens, *(ii)* to identify the illegal migrants living in different parts of the country and *(iii)* to cheek further occurrence of illegal migration from Bangladesh.
5. Bihit Bidhan Kisha, Research Scholar in the Delhi School of Social Work, Binoy Reang, a lawyer from the Law Faculty, University of Delhi and Stephen N of the Jawharlal Nehru University are some of such students, who told the scholar about the same, expressing their discontent and dissatisfaction over the Government of India's policy in dealing with the problem of illegal immigration in the Northeast.
6. For instance, Mr. Suhas Chakma, Director, Asian Center for Human Rights, New Delhi is one who believes that instead of being selective, the Government of India needs to have a pragmatic approach to prove its seriousness in dealing with the problem of illegal immigration. Mr. Bijoy Kumar Wrangkal, President of INPT, and Debabrata Kaloi, ex Chairman of the TTADC argue that tribal insurgency in Tripura can not be permanently solved so long as the feeling of xenophobia is not decimated from the indigenous tribal communities of the state, a situation to arise needs checkmating illegal immigration.
7. 'Just War Theory' justifies direct military intervention, if necessary, on humanitarian ground to defeat a regime that unleash a reign of terror in the country with virtual breakdown of law and order situation and threaten international security. Michael Waltzer, *Millenium series lecture in the University of Delhi*, organized by the Department of Political Science, University of Delhi, 2003. Also, see, John Baylis et al., *The Globalization of World Politics*, op. cit, pp. 221-24.

Bibliography

Primary Sources

I. Documents, Reports

1. A Memorandum, submitted by the Chittagong Hill Tracts Peoples' Association (CHTPA) to the Committee of India's Constituent Assembly, February 15, 1947.
2. A Millennium series lecture by Michel Waltzer in the University of Delhi, organized by the Department of Political Science, University of Delhi, 2003.
3. The CHTPA's letter to Dr. Syamaprasad Mukerjee, January 24, 1948.
4. The Charter of the Modified Five Points Demand of the PCJSS, a publication of the Department of Information and Publicity of the PCJSS, 15 August 1997.
5. Manik Rao Hotlia Gavit, Deputy Minister in

the Home affairs, Government of India on statistical figures about Muslim population in West Bengal and the Northeast India, *The Rajya Sabha Session*, 18 March 2005.

6. The Population Census Report of Tripura, 1991, Statistical Department, Government of Tripura.
7. The statistical figures about the expenditures incurred for maintenance of the six refugee camps in the South Tripura until the repatriation of the refugees in 1997, Department of Relief and Rehabilitation, Government of Tripura.

II. Interviews and personal interactions and e-mails

1. Babatosh Dewan, a senior leader of undivided PCJSS. He was the Secretary General of the PCJSS until the outbreak of the civil war between the members of Shanti Bahini in 1983.
2. Priti Kumar Chakma, a senior member of the undivided PCJSS.
3. Kali Madhav Chakma, a senior leader and founding member of the PCJSS.
4. Gopal Chakma, a retired RAW officer of India.
5. Subir Bhaumik, B.B.C. Eastern India Correspondent.
6. Bibhuti Bhusan Nandi, a retired senior officer of RAW and a columnist.
7. Mr. Suhas Chakma, Director, Asian centre for Human Rights and Asian Indigenous and Tribal Peoples Network, New Delhi.
8. Goutam Chakma, a senior Lecturer in the

Department of Political Science, University of Tripura.

9. Mrinal Khanti Chakma, a research scholar in the Department of Political Science, Rabindrabarati University, Kolkata. He also served as the Coordinator of the CHT Japan Committee for few years.
10. Subimal Chakma, President of the Committee for Citizenship Rights of the Chakmas in Arunachal Pradesh.
11. Bihita Bidhan Kisha, a research scholar in the Delhi School of Social Work, University of Delhi.
12. Binoy Reang, a lawyer, who was graduated from the Department of Law, University of Delhi.
13. Sanjoy Chakma, once a senior leader and founding member of the UPDF.

Secondary Sources

I. Books

1. Anderson, Surah (ed.), c, d, *View From the South: The Effect of Globalization and the WTO on the Third World Countries*, San Francisco: IFG.
2. Agarwal, M.M., 1996, *Ethnicity, Culture and Nationalism in North-East India*, Indus International, New Delhi.
3. Bandyopadhyaya, Jayantanuja, 1991, *The Making of India's Foreign Policy*, Calcutta: Allied Publishers
4. Banerji, Arun Kumar, (et. al.), 2001, *Peoples Republic of China at Fifty*, New Delhi: Lancers' Book.

5. Baylis, John (et. al.), 2001, *The Globalization of World Politics*, Oxford: Oxford University Press.

6. Bhaumik, Subir, (et. al.) 1997, *Living on the Edge: Essays on the Chittagong Hill Tracts*, Kathmandu: South Asia Forum for Human Rights.

7. ————1996, *Insurgent Crossfire: Northeast India*, Lancer Publishers: New Delhi.

8. ————*The Troubled Periphery : Crisis of India's Northeast*, a forthcoming book to be published by Penguin.

9. Bose, Sumantra, 1994, *States, Nations, Sovereignty: Srilanka, India and the Tamil Eelam Movement*, New Delhi: Sage Publications.

10. Chari, P.R. (ed.), 2000, Perspective *on national security In South Asia: In Search of a New Paradigm*, New Delhi: Monohar.

11. Commission, The CHT, 1995, Life *is not ours: Land and Rights in the CHT, Bangladesh*, Netherlands.

12. Debnath, Jayanta, 2001, *Santrasklanta Tripura*, Dainik Sambad Publishers: Agartala.

13. Dewan, Aditya Kumar, 1990, *Class and Ethnicity in the Hills of Bangladesh*, an unpublished Ph.D. dissertation paper, Mc-Gill University.

14. Donnelly, Jack, 2000, *Realism and International Relations*, Cambridge: Cambridge University Press.

15. Ganguly, Sumit, 1999, *The Origin of War in South Asia: Indo- Pakistani Conflict Since 1947*, Vision Books: New Delhi.

16. Ghoshal, H.D. (et.al), 2000, *International Relations*, New Delhi: Unique Publishers.

17. Hirst, Paul, 2001, *War and Power in the 21st Century*, Cambridge: Polity Press.

18. Iftekharuzzam (ed.), 1998, *Ethnicity and Constitutional Reform in South Asia*, New Delhi: Monohar.

19. Mallick, Ross, 1998, *Ethnicity and Human Rights in South Asia*, New Delhi: Sage Publication.

20. Mohsin, Amena, 1997, *The Politics of Nationalism: The Case of the Chittagong Hill Tracts, Bangladesh*, Dhaka: The University Press Limited.

21. Morghenthau, Hans.J., 1985, *Politics Among Nations*, New Delhi: Kalyani Publishers.

22. Mukerji, Saradindu, 2000, *Subjects, Citizens and Refugees: Tragedy in the Chittagong Hill Tracts (1947-1998)*, New Delhi: Indian Centre for the Study of Forced Migration.

23. Narang, A.S., 1997, *Indian Government and Politics*, New Delhi: Gitanjali Publishing House.

24. P. Sahadevan, P. (ed.), 2001, *Conflict and Peacemaking in South Asia*, New Delhi: Lancer's Book.

25. Ranganathan, C. V. and C. Khanna, Vinod, 2000, *India and China: The Way Ahead After 'Mao's India War'*, New Delhi: Har Anand.

26. Ritchie, Mark (et.al), 1999, *WTO and the Globalization of Food Insecurity*, San Francisco: International Forum on Globalization (IFG).

27. Roy, Rajkumari Chandra Kalindi, 2000, *Land Rights of the Indigenous Peoples of the Chittagong Hill Tracts, Bangladesh*, Copenhagen: IWGIA Document No. 99.

28. Shiva, Vandana (et.al), 1994, *The Future of Progress: Reflection on Environment and Development*, Dehradun: Natraj.

29. Stein, Arthur A., 1990, *Why Nations Cooperate*, Ithaca: Cornel University Press.

30. Upreti, B.C. (ed.), *SAARC: Dynamics of Regional Cooperation in South Asia*, New Delhi: Vedams Books (P) Ltd.

II. Journal, Newspapers, and Documents

1. *American Journal of International Law*, Vol. 92, Issue 3 July 1998.

2. *Millennium*, vol. 25, No.3 1996.

3. *Journal of Commonwealth and Comparative Politics*, Vol. XXXI, No. 3, 1993.

4. *Transnational*, Ardsley NY, 2000.

5. *Vision*, Rangamati, 15 June 1995.

6. *Population Transfer and Implantation of Bengali Settlers: The Threat of Survival of the Jumma People*, New Delhi: Jumma People Network (JNP) of South Asia Coordination Section, 6 April 1999.

7. *The booklet on drop out rate*, published by the Directorate of School Education, Government of Tripura, 2003.

8. *Ajker Kagaj*, Dhaka, 27 June 2002.

9. *Bhorer Kagaj*, Dhaka, a leading Bengali daily of Bangladesh, Dhaka, 20 May 2002.

10. *Dainik Sambad*, Agartala, 19 March 2005.

11. *The Dainik Sangram*, Dhaka, 1 April 2002.

12. The *Hindustan Times*, New Delhi, 1 December 2002.

13. *India Today*, December 9, 2002.

14. *The Statesman*, Kolkata, 1 November 2001

15. *The Statesman*, Kolkata, 30 November 2002.

16. *The Swadikar*, a periodical news bulletin of the UPDF, July 2001.

17. The *Syandan Patrika*, Agartala, 19 March 2005.

18. The *Telegraph*, Kolkata, 12 May, 2003.

III. Websites

1. www.aitpn.org/research.html
2. www.amidatrust.com/CHT_update_2.htm.
3. http:// www.anglefire.com/ab/jumma.religion.html.
4. http:// www.asiapacificms.com/articles/bangladesh_terror/.
5. http:// www.saag.org/papers3/paper235.html.
6. http://www.satp.org/satporgtp/countries/bangladesh/.
7. http://www.tehelka.com/channels/currentaffairs/2002/mar/25/ca03250.
8. www.updfcht.org.

Abhi. 5900
10/01/11, 2 copy)